MW00344127

AS TIME GOES BY
ONE MARINE'S STORY

JB Redus

RED ENGINE
PRESS
PRINTED IN THE USA

As Time Goes By: One Marine's Story
JB Redus

WITHOUT LIMITING THE RIGHTS UNDER COPYRIGHT RESERVED BELOW, NO PART OF THIS PUBLICATION MAY BE REPRODUCED, STORED IN OR INTRODUCED INTO RETRIEVAL SYSTEM, OR TRANSMITTED, IN ANY FORM OR BY ANY MEANS (ELECTRONIC, MECHANICAL, PHOTOCOPYING, RECORDING, OR OTHERWISE), INCLUDING MEDIUMS NOT YET INVENTED AT TIME OF PUBLICATION, WITHOUT PRIOR WRITTEN PERMISSION FROM BOTH THE COPYRIGHT OWNER AND THE PUBLISHER OF THIS BOOK.

HARDCOVER ISBN: 978-1-943267-90-3

PAPERBACK ISBN: 978-1-943267-91-0

LIBRARY OF CONGRESS CONTROL NUMBER: 2021951616

TEXT COPYRIGHT © 2021 BY JB REDUS

FIRST EDITION ~ DECEMBER 2021

10 9 8 7 6 5 4 3 2 1

PUBLISHED BY RED ENGINE PRESS, PITTSBURGH, PENNSYLVANIA USA

PRINTED IN THE USA ~ ALL RIGHTS RESERVED.

DEDICATION

To my wife, Cherry and to our children; James Brady, Rachel, Cherry Beth, and Megan.

WHAT OTHERS ARE SAYING

I AM SO PLEASED JB HAS written his story. It will enlighten and encourage all who read it. War is Hell and his experiences spell it out clearly. No one can understand the tragic things that occurred in Viet Nam unless they have been there. JB's story will take you as close as you want.

~ *CHUCK BOWMAN. HEAD Football Coach at NEO A&M College in Miami, Oklahoma. 1967-1971*

* * *

I COULDN'T PUT JB's book down. I was shocked at his memory for details. Names, places, and dates were as vivid as the colors in my watercolor palette. The Sap Green of the Huey helicopters, the Payne's Grey of my M-16, or the Burnt Sienna of the wood on my M-14—that was the weapon I started with on arrival in 1968. JB weaves in and out of a killer ambush memory like it was yesterday's news and you can feel the sweat and taste the blood when it's over. He finally gets back to Tulsa where we played football together, with all his limbs intact. But he is a different man now—we all are after that war. His is a story well told and worth the read—you will come out the other end touched by the heat.

~ *DOUG CLAYBOURNE, Film Producer*

* * *

FROM ONE JARHEAD TO another JB, first and foremost, thank you for your service. The story surrounding the combat mission in Vietnam has never been truly revealed. Your account needs to be shared with every American. 60,000 lives lost for what? As I have written on other occasions when reflecting back on yet another ill-advised war, police action or intervention...Just another check written by old, fat, and partisan politicians which members of America's military ranks are expected to cash. Well done, Marine! *Semper Fi*

~ *RUSTY FLEMING, USMC*

* * *

JAMES BRUCE REDUS TElls of a boy growing up in Texas and Oklahoma then making the decision to join the United States Marine Corps, a decision that would change his life forever. As a Marine, JB tells of his time on Sea Duty then eventually being assigned to serve with an infantry unit in Vietnam where he would be injured in the line of duty. He shares with us his time in recovery and his life moving forward. *As Time Goes By* is the story of James Bruce Redus, in his own words.

~ *CPL E BEESLEY USMC RET.*

* * *

A RIVETING DESCRIPTION of war through the eyes of one Marine.
~ *D. BRUCE HOWELL, Tulsa Public School Superintendent (retired) and Author*

* * *

ON THE AFTERNOON OF October 23rd, 1983, I came home from school. I was ten years old. Usually the house was quiet. Dad worked nights and Mom was at work. I tried to be quiet as I unlocked the door and came inside. Dad was sitting in a chair, his face was in his hands, and he was obviously upset. The TV was on. Something about a bombing in Beirut. I had no idea what was going on. As I spoke with my father, he told me 220 marines, eighteen sailors, and three soldiers were killed. Again, he was visibly upset. I asked if he knew any of them. He said, "No." I asked if there was someone there we possibly would know. He said, "No." It was that day I decided to join the Marine Corps someday. This man whom I had never seen crying or upset, was sobbing over men he did not know but were Marines. At ten years old, I did not, but I thought I understood the word, "brother". Dad never shielded me from his thoughts after that. He was training me, even though I did not know it. He was preparing me. I owe all I have accomplished and learned from this man. I am a former Marine, retired Fire Captain, Flight Nurse/Paramedic and it all started in that moment. The moment I learned a man can have such a feeling for men he did not know just by being a member of the greatest fighting force the world has ever known. I am beyond proud to call that man my father.
~ *CPL BRADY REDUS RN,CEN, NREMT-P*

TABLE OF CONTENTS

INTRODUCTION

"These are times that try men's souls; the summer soldier and the sunshine patriot will, in this crisis, shrink from the service of his country; but he that stands it now, deserves the love and thanks of man and woman. Tyranny, like hell, is not easily conquered; yet we have this consolation with us, that the harder the conflict, the more glorious the triumph."

~ Thomas Paine

Writing a book is not an easy task. It takes a great deal of planning and preparation. I wrote notes to myself in a tablet next to my favorite chair—names, experiences, places, times. It all came back to me. Outlines, rough drafts were written only to be thrown into the trash. It was important for me that I get it right, that what I wrote was the truth, written in a way the reader could feel the experience, absorb the sadness, joy, triumph, and fear. I changed some of the names because I didn't want families to read about the death or disappointment of a loved one.

Throughout the book you'll read about people who've made a difference in my life— individuals who made me who I am today. They built my character, one stone at a time. Looking back, it's clear to me I needed them a lot more than they needed me. Mistakes were made, coupled with bad decisions. They were opportunities to learn, to recognize them when our paths cross again.

Joining the Corps was a decision I made years earlier. It was a test. I couldn't see myself being anywhere else. Please note there were times I wished I was somewhere else.

Read on.

Semper Fi

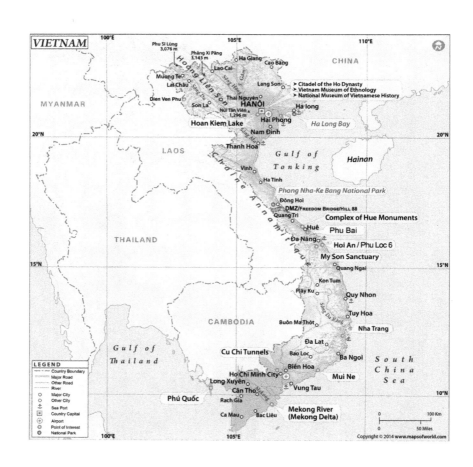

1

It's Clean Until It Hits the Ground

There's a battle between two wolves inside us. One is evil, the other is good. Which one wins? The one you feed. ~ Cherokee Tale

IT WAS A BEAUTIFUL DAY. The sun warmed our faces as we loaded onto the bus at Horno Ridge, Camp Pendleton. Our duffel bags stood up between our legs. We settled in for the ride to the Marine Air Station at El Toro. Everyone was quiet. It reminded me of the bus ride I took from the airport in San Diego to MCRD, where a Marine sergeant loomed over us as we stopped at a checkpoint before entering the gate. This time we didn't *have* to keep quiet, eyeballs straight ahead, sitting at attention. To a man, we thought about what lay ahead just a few days away.

Somehow destiny had brought us there. We had two things in common—we had all volunteered, and we all wanted to be Marines. There was no cutting up, no joking, and no rubbernecking. Within hours, we would be on a flight to a place that before had seemed so distant, so far off. Reality stared us in the face. Our time had come.

At El Toro we were loaded into a World Airways jet. As we taxied down the runway, I glanced out the window. We quickly climbed to gain airspace. The wheels made a loud thump as they folded into the undercarriage.

I thought about closing my eyes, but I wasn't ready to relax. A couple of Marines in the seats in front of me tried to get the stewardess to lean way over to ask her a question or to get a cold drink. The four stewardesses were young and pretty. They wore high boots and miniskirts. If the Marines could get her to lean over far enough, the Marines in the seats across from them would get a look at her long legs and panties. This worked for a while until the stewardess figured it out and squatted down and passed drinks to them. I don't think the stewardesses really minded that much. They knew where we were going, and for some of us, it would be their last trip.

Hours later we landed in Hawaii. They pulled the jet into a hanger. We were told, "You can get out of the plane and stretch your legs but do not wander off."

They had vending machines in the office, so we helped ourselves. As a lady walked by, I heard her ask someone at the counter, "What are all of these Marines doing here?"

The lady behind the counter told her, "They are going to Vietnam."

The lady who asked the question responded, "I'm sure they don't mind."

I never understood what she meant, but it didn't matter. It just didn't matter. It wasn't important.

After about an hour, we loaded back on the plane. They pulled the big jet outside the hanger, and we were airborne. Our next stop was Camp Schwab, named for a Marine who was posthumously awarded the Medal of Honor during the battle for Okinawa.

That part of the flight was longer. I decided to close my eyes.

What happened in my life that led me to this moment? Is my life more precious than any of the other young men on this flight? If I ask God to spare me, would he hear me?

It's all there, even though I've tried to forget.

* * *

I grew up in Houston, Texas. During the summer months the humidity was stifling. There was never any wind unless there was a hurricane in the Gulf. We lived in a small house just off S. Park Blvd. The homes were pretty much the same. They had siding, were about 950 square feet, three small bedrooms, one bath, a small living room and kitchen, and a one-car garage. We had a washing machine, but clothes were hung out to dry on a line in the backyard.

Two long strips of concrete made their way to the street with grass and weeds between them. There was a Jewish family down the street and two Mexican families just around the corner. Most of the families were middle class or lower middle class.

At Easter we hid colored eggs. My father brought home a couple baby chickens, covered with a red or blue dye. They never lived very long. My sister and I took the bus to Vacation Bible School during the summer. I went mostly for the free snow cones at break and learned to memorize the books of the Bible (New Testament), if only to please my teacher.

There was a large pipe next to a bridge we crossed on our way to school. We took turns walking across the pipe, showing off. Going under the bridge, we rolled up pieces of newspaper and build campfires, or took rocks and dammed up the stream.

In early June 1954, my family prepared for our annual trip to Oklahoma. Every year, all six of us loaded into our 1950 Oldsmobile for the twelve-hour drive to Shawnee.

Back then, there were no superhighways. It was two lanes all the way. The speed limit was sixty miles-per-hour. We had no air conditioning. The windows were down. I remember going through every small town along the way: Crockett, Bowie, Denison, etc.

My father had put two cases of *Pearl* beer in the trunk. Oklahoma was a dry state back then. The beer was for my Uncle Lonnie.

The night before we were supposed to leave, my father was cleaning a part of the car engine with gasoline. Our dog stepped on the edge of the pan, spilling the gas across the garage floor. The gas spread under the hot water tank, and the tank exploded.

A good part of the garage was in flames, but the fire department got there in time to save the house. The fire was out, but most of the damage was in the garage. It never made it up the wall or into the attic.

My father had a few third-degree burns and had to spend the night in the hospital.

Several of my aunts and uncles stopped by to lend a hand. The fire department told my mother the house was safe—we could spend the night there, but the smell of smoke would linger for some time.

I climbed into bed and fell asleep. Then something woke me. Someone was hollering. I sat up and saw my mother and one of my uncles standing in the bathroom's doorway. They were using words I didn't understand.

I heard my name, then my mother said, "I never wanted him."

As a seven-year-old child it was hard to understand what I was hearing. I cried myself to sleep.

The next morning when I awoke, my clothes were packed. My mother told me I was going to Port Arthur to stay with Aunt Sis. When I asked why and for how long, she ignored me.

I stayed at my aunt's and uncle's house for three months, not returning until the middle of September. I didn't hear from my parents during that time. I figured they were busy getting the house repaired.

When my aunt and uncle took me home, I ran up the driveway. My mother was sitting in the rocking chair, still in her pajamas.

She wore a brown robe. When I got to her, I stopped. She sat there, staring at me. A few seconds went by. I said nothing, then ran to the side of the house to see my brother and sisters.

The next day my older sister (who was a couple of grades ahead of me) took me to the office at Kelso Elementary. She explained why I was starting back to school so late. Once everything was cleared up, my sister showed me where my classroom was and left.

I was starting the second grade.

* * *

In 1959, we moved to Spring Branch, which was a suburb of Houston—just off the Katy Highway. The house was larger and there were plenty of woods around to explore.

I borrowed a friend's Benjamin pump that shot one pellet at a time. You had to pump it up with a wooden handle below the barrel to fire it again.

There were big drainage ditches down from the house. After school, I went looking for water moccasins. It was my experience moccasins were an aggressive snake. If you wounded them with the first shot, they moved toward you. Several times I ran along the ditch, pellets in my mouth, pumping that Benjamin to get off a second shot. Sometimes I had to put two pellets in the snake's head to stop it.

Prince, my male beagle and I took to the woods together. It was great, just the two of us out there hunting together.

At the time, I had no idea looking for signs of animals and hunting in the woods would be a skill I would use later in my life as a Marine. I would be hunting a far more dangerous animal, *man*.

* * *

I was fourteen in the summer of '61. With school out, most of my time was spent mowing lawns and washing dishes one night a week (Saturday) at Brener's Steakhouse.

If I didn't have my friend's Benjamin pump, all I could do was walk along a branch creek and sting a swamp rabbit or a squirrel. My BB gun didn't have the velocity to bring 'em down.

It didn't really matter. The whole idea was to be out there, feel the warmth of the sun on my face, sweat running down my neck, gun in my hands, and walk for hours.

I was going to talk to my ol' man to see if maybe he could buy a power mower. It was getting old real quick using the reel type mower, especially when I had to make two passes over the same ground. Using a file to sharpen the blades didn't seem to last long after doing two yards in one day.

I milled around in the garage to catch him when he drove up.

"Hey, Dad. Do you think we could get a gas-powered mower? I'll pay for the gas and oil."

"Now what do I need a gas mower for? I've got you," he said as he walked into the house.

He thought it was funny. I didn't.

The next morning after I finished mowing our yard, I decided to walk over to the city park—about a mile from the house and stop by Roger's house to see what he was up to.

The park was beautiful. It was heavily wooded, and you could smell the pine trees.

I knocked on his door several times, but nobody was home. I walked back across the street onto the shoulder and headed home.

It wasn't long until I heard a car honk as it pulled up beside me. Looking over my left shoulder, I recognized the driver. It was Tommie.

"Hey, kid. You want a ride? Come on, get in."

"Sure, Tommie."

I met Tommie a few weeks before school let out. His yellow convertible was hard to miss. The rumor around the neighborhood was he had spent time in a reform school in Texas called Gatesville. He was one of the local toughs, or what we called under our breath, "hard dicks".

"What you been up to, kid?"

"Not much. Mowing lawns and working down at the steak house, washing dishes one night a week."

"Man, that sounds too much like work to me!"

I nodded my head.

As I gave him directions, Tommie dangled his left arm out the window and steered with his right hand. On the steering wheel was a large knob. It was white and looked like a piece of crystal. He turned the wheel with quick circles holding onto that knob. The force of the turns leaned me to one side and then the other.

As I was getting out of the car I said, "Thanks, Tommie."

"That's okay, kid. See you around!"

He took off like someone was chasing him. I heard his tires scream as he made the turn at the end of the block.

As I walked toward the house, I thought about the zip gun in Tommie's glove box he showed me.

"Hey, kid. You want to see something? Open that box up. Just push the button and take a look."

I opened the glove box. Inside was what looked like a piece of steel pipe with a piece of wood attached to it. Several large thick rubber bands hung loose.

"Go ahead, kid. Take it out. Go ahead. It's not gonna hurt you. That's right, hold it by that piece of wood. That's like a pistol grip. You see that nail? That's the firing pin. It's like a pistol. If you can get it to fire, you gotta be real close. You know what I mean? You gotta be *real* close."

"Did you make it?"

"Yeah. I learned how at that school I went to, up at the Gates."

I put his zip gun back in the glove box.

"You ever fired it?"

"No, not yet. I got a buddy of mine that's gonna show me. You know, give me help with it."

As I walked through the front door, it crossed my mind—Tommie was going to live fast, love hard, and die young. He probably wouldn't have it any other way.

About two weeks later, a friend of mine invited me to go to the drive-in with his parents.

Between features, the two of us decided to go to the concession stand. The money I had made was burning a hole in my pocket.

As we walked back to the car, I heard a voice.

"Hey, kid! Hey kid, over here. Yeah, you. Come here. I got something you gotta see."

I recognized the voice. It was Tommie.

As we got closer, I saw he had several of his friends with him. They were standing behind and to the left of a station wagon parked in the back row. As we got closer, Tommie came up to me and put his hand on my shoulder.

"Come over here. I want to show you something special. Here, let your friend hold your drink. You're not gonna need that. I have a surprise for you."

He took me by the arm and led me to the back of the car.

It was backed up to a sheet-metal fence. The top and bottom car gates were open.

The second feature hadn't started yet, and it was dark. I heard a voice.

"Come here, honey!"

Tommie and one of his friends picked me up and tossed me in the back of the station wagon. I landed on a young girl.

She looked a little heavy. All she was wearing was a blouse, unbuttoned and opened in the front.

"Come here, baby. Let me help you. You don't need those pants on."

She undid my jeans and pushed down my underwear, while Tommie and his friends pulled on my pants' legs.

It happened very fast. I was nervous. Sweat beads ran down my face. She grabbed ahold of my *twig*.

Nothing happened.

All I remember hearing was, "Come on, baby, come on. I'll help you."

By that time, my jeans and underwear were around my ankles. I heard Tommie and his friends hollering and laughing.

Still nothing happened.

It couldn't have been more than a few minutes, but it seemed longer.

The girl finally spoke up, "Get him off me. Get this pencil dick off me! Go on, get out of here. Tommie, get this pencil dick off me!"

With that, I slid out the back, pulled up my pants, and quickly walked away.

Tommie and his friends laughed and hollered. I couldn't walk fast enough.

I turned to Toby as we headed toward his parents' car.

"Don't you tell anyone about this. I'm not kidding. Don't you say a word to anyone."

"Heck man, it was dark. Those guys were crowded around the car. I could barely see what was happening. They were so loud I couldn't hear what was going on inside. When we get back to the car, if my parents ask why we were gone so long, we'll tell 'em we met up with friends at the concession stand. Alright?"

"Yeah, that sounds good."

"Here. Here's your pop back."

As time passed, I didn't see Tommie again for quite a while. Then one afternoon, Mike and I were walking along the road. Tommie blew by, waving and hollering—

"Hey, pencil dick," laughing hilariously.

Mike asked me, "What did he say?"

"I don't know. I didn't get it either."

That was the last time I ever saw Tommie. The word around the neighborhood was he had moved. Other people said he had another brush with the cops.

As for me, I hoped I would never see Tommie again, but I did like his car.

* * *

It wasn't until I turned sixteen that I started looking for serious work—no more mowing yards or washing dishes at Brener's Steakhouse on the weekends.

I walked about a mile-and-a-half to a *Conoco* service station just off Gesner Road. When I talked to the owner, things went well until he asked me, "Can you drive a standard shift?"

I lied, "Yes, sir. I can."

The truth was I knew about the H pattern. I knew about the clutch and when to push on the gas. I was sure I could do it. I had seen my friends drive a stick shift. I needed that job.

What I didn't realize at the time, he wanted me to start right then.

"Get in the service truck and follow Samson. He's going to take a customer's car back to him. Then, the two of you come back and I'll teach you how to grease a car," he said.

"Okay. Yes, sir."

I got into the old service truck. The keys were in it. I released the brake, pushed in the clutch, and put the stick in neutral. The starter was in the floorboard. I pressed it with my left foot.

The engine roared to life. I breathed a sigh of relief. *So far so good.*

Pressing on the clutch, I found reverse. I gave it some gas. I let out the clutch, and the truck began to move.

Then, the truck died.

I thought, *I've got to give it more gas.*

I nervously looked out the side window. Samson had his head out the car window, just shaking his head.

"Come on, boy!"

I was more determined. I gave it more gas and eased out the clutch. It died a second time. I was determined to make it the next time. I started it up, eased out on the clutch, and gave it more gas.

What I didn't realize a hump was behind the front wheels. Each time I moved the truck, I couldn't get over the hump.

The third time, I gave it more gas and let out the clutch more slowly. I gave it more gas, and the tires screamed. Off we went.

I backed into the building with a loud bang. The truck died, and I didn't dare look at Samson.

As I slowly looked over my left shoulder, the station owner was walking toward me.

My first thought was, *He's going to fire me, there's going to be yelling.*

The building was probably damaged, and I was sure he knew I had lied to him. As I sat there waiting for him, he stuck his head in the door window.

"Are you alright?"

"Yes, sir!"

"Why don't you drive the car and let Samson drive the truck."

"Yes, sir."

I couldn't believe what I heard. He wasn't going to fire me. I got out of the truck.

As I passed Samson, he said, "Now you lookie here, boy. You follow me and don't lose me. You got dat?"

"Yes, sir. I won't lose you. I mean, no, sir. I won't lose you."

Samson and I became great friends.

Afterward, he suggested we go across the street. There was a shopping center with a large parking lot. He taught me to drive a standard shift. I was a good student. With his patience, it didn't take long for me to get the hang of it. The two of us worked well together.

Samson was about six feet tall, slender build, and as black as coal. He was a proud man and my friend.

"You takes a man's money, you earns your pay."

We both walked home each evening. There was plenty of time to talk.

When I asked him a question like, "Are you going to buy a car?" His favorite answer was, "Got that to git."

Samson was a godsend. I remember something he told me that has always stayed with me.

"Don't matter what happens to a person in life, it's how you deals with it that's important."

I think about him often.

The owner of the gas station eventually sold it, so Samson and I were out of a job. We said our good-byes, and I went down the street to Bolton's Burgers looking for work.

Mr. Bolton hired me at $.50 an hour—less than I had been making. But the real benefit was I could eat all I wanted. I had a good work ethic. Samson had seen to that.

After a short time, I learned how to cook hamburgers, fry French fries, make malts, and pour in the liquid to make ice cream.

Mr. Bolton worked for a Plymouth dealership selling cars. The hamburger stand was a side job. He began to leave me there more often by myself. Believe it or not, you can get tired of hamburgers and malts after a while. I think he knew that.

It was 1963, and the sign out front flashed off-and-on, BOLTON'S BURGERS, FIVE FOR A DOLLAR. We were always busy.

One night, a large black man came to the window and gave me his order. When I looked up, I couldn't help but notice he had a shiny quarter in each of his earlobes. I tried not to stare.

There were a lot of colorful people, especially bikers and some of the local toughs.

Mr. Bolton liked to drink and shared his booze. His wife frequently came by during the day when he wasn't there, to go through the big aluminum milk pails looking for his liquor. It was a real circus at times but an interesting place to work.

Sometimes at closing, he gave me two cans of beer to drink on my way home. Back then, there were no tabs on beer cans. You had to open each can with a church key.

I was careful not to spill any of it on me so I didn't walk into the house smelling like beer.

There was a park about halfway home. If I made it there, I didn't have to worry about the police or cars going by. It was quiet. I sat on a bench and finished the second can.

One night as I walked home at about twelve o'clock in the evening, a dark blue car suddenly pulled up beside me. The driver rolled down the window.

I recognized the man. He owned a couple of stores in Spring Branch. The word about him was he was "queer".

He smiled, "Hello. You need a lift?"

"No thanks. I don't have much further to go."

"Come on. Hop in."

I took a good look at him, a little hesitant. Then, I thought I could take him if he started anything. As I got into the car, it smelled as if he had broken a bottle of aftershave on the floorboard.

Nothing much was said as we rode along.

"Turn here, then make a left. You can stop just up there—the house with the two planters on the driveway," I told him.

As I was about to step out, I said, "Thanks."

As I turned the door handle, he said, "Hey, hang on a minute. I want to show you something. Take a look at what I've got here. Have you ever seen anything like this before?"

The door was open. As I looked back, he shoved a handful of photos toward me. At first glance the photos were men and women in different sexual positions. Then, men with men in different sexual positions.

As I casually glanced, I said, "Yeah, I've seen this one," and so on. The door was open, so I stepped out and placed the photos on the seat. "Thanks again for the ride."

I got my key out and walked into the house. Once in the house, I went over to the drapes and barely pulled them back to see if he was still there.

He was.

When I got ready for bed, I went into the living room and pulled back the drapes again. He was still there, so I checked the door to make sure it was locked. I went to bed. It had been a long day and I was tired.

From that time on as I walked home, I watched for him. If I thought I saw him, I crossed the street and into someone's yard. Our paths never crossed again.

The Artisan Well

It was a Saturday in the middle of September 1963, and we had a game to play against Lamar's Junior Varsity. Texans took their high school football very seriously. Even though it was junior varsity, we still had a nice crowd.

After the game, Tim, Jimmy, and I decided to take off and go out to the rice fields close to the Addick's Spillway.

The farmers had tanks (ponds) that irrigated the fields. Each tank had a diesel motor hooked to a pump that drew water from the artisan wells. A large pipe about a foot in diameter stuck out over the tank. About once every hour, a timer started up the motor and clean, cold ground water came flowing out.

We parked the car, got rid of our clothes, and dove in. It was wonderful to dive in on a hot and humid day—such freedom. While Tim and I swam and jumped off the pipe, unbeknown to us, Jimmy snuck off and grabbed our clothes.

He got to his car and began to drive off, honking the horn. We hadn't missed him until we heard the horn. We hadn't missed our clothes, either.

As we climbed out and ran naked toward the car, Jimmy laughed and waved. He drove just enough to keep us from reaching the car. It continued for about a hundred yards to the asphalt road.

On the road, he kept yelling, "Come on, fellers. I'll wait on you."

That was a lie.

As Tim and I ran to the hot road, not wearing a stitch, an old pickup suddenly came toward us. Tim and I ran to get off the road and over a barbed-wire fence to hide in brush.

It's a very careful move getting through barbed wire—getting your "biscuits" over the fence without causing any sort of hang up.

Two elderly people, a man and a woman slowly drove by, watching us hunkered down in the sparse brush. And, we were watching them.

As they drove away, Jimmy backed up laughing and waving. "Come on. Get out of there. Come on."

We carefully got through the fence one more time. Being barefooted, we maneuvered through the small rocks and hot asphalt.

As we three drove off together, we made jokes and laughed about the old couple. We wondered if they ever saw us again, would they recognize us.

* * *

It was 1964. I was seventeen and my family had moved to Oklahoma. School was out for the summer.

My mother told me, "Go find a job and don't come back until you've got one."

Just one block from our house, new homes were being built. It seemed a good place to start. That's where I met John Hickey.

John was a supervisor for David Dillon, a local builder. When I told him I wanted a job, he said the only thing he had was cleaning up after the framer, the sheet rockers, plumbers, and electricians. The pay was one dollar an hour. I took it.

They had an old truck to haul off everything that couldn't be burned. I thought of Samson and the old service truck in Spring Branch.

Sometimes things happened for a reason, and you don't realize it at the time.

John was a country boy. He was always good for a laugh or a good story. [I hope he is well.]

That summer, David the owner of the construction company told me he appreciated my hard work. We got along well.

I usually worked until it was almost dark and then walked home. One night when I got to the screen door, it was locked. I rang the doorbell and waited.

My mother came to the door, opened it, and just stood there behind the screen door.

"The screen door is locked."

"You don't live here anymore."

Her words caught me by surprise. I asked her, "What do you mean, I don't live here?"

"You don't live here anymore. Your clothes are wrapped up in that sheet by the door."

I went through the clothes checking to see if everything was there.

"Is my radio in here?"

She shut the door. After a few minutes passed, she came back.

"Step back away from the screen door." She unlocked the door, opened it, and tossed my radio onto the yard.

I walked over to pick it up.

That was when my father stepped out. That was when he told me, "I'm not your father."

"I know that. I've known it for years."

Through the years, I overheard my relatives talking. Over time, I put the pieces together, thinking at some point it would all come to a head. It would seem that day had come.

Putting my radio inside the sheet, I faced both of them.

As I turned to walk away, he hollered my real father's name. It went in one ear and out the other. I didn't need to hear it. It wasn't important to me.

As I turned the corner by the garage, my eyes glassed up a little bit, then they quickly dried up. It was not the time to feel sorry for myself.

I have money for food, but where am I going to live? Staying in one of the partially build houses may be alright for a day or so. Then I have to think of something else.

David, the man I worked for lived in one of his show homes. He was going through a divorce. *Maybe he will take me in.*

I walked the two blocks to his house and rang the doorbell.

"What are you doing here?"

"My parents have kicked me out. I need a place to stay."

"Come on in. You can stay in the bedroom upstairs. I don't know how long I'm gonna be here, but you are welcome."

"Thanks, David."

"Here, let me help you with your things."

"No, that's alright. I've got it. Where's my room?"

"Upstairs and to the left. I've got extra towels you can use and tomorrow we'll see if we can find you something to sleep on."

"Thanks, David."

David and I didn't see that much of each other. I tried to stay out of his way. In the evening, I ate at a restaurant on Sheridan, went back to the house, and went to sleep. I wanted to be as little trouble to him as possible.

After a few weeks, my stepfather drove up to a house I was working on and rolled down his car window.

"How are you doing?"

"Fine."

"Do you need anything?"

"Nope."

"You wouldn't tell me even if you did, would you?"

"Nope."

He drove off.

It was late June, 1964. David and I were doing just fine. The weeks went by until late in July. David told me he was going to get an apartment. I would have to find someplace else to stay.

I hated to ask, but with football starting in a couple of weeks, it was time to see about going home. I waited on the side of the garage at the house until my stepfather drove up.

"I need to come back home."

His reaction was a surprise. He didn't give me any trouble. I had already decided if there was any trouble, I would walk away. Where? I didn't know. I would just walk away.

"Come on, let's go in the house."

I said nothing to anyone. I went to my old bedroom I had shared with my brother, laid down, and went to sleep. Later when I woke, I went into the kitchen, got something to eat, and again said nothing to anyone.

Getting up at 6:30 the next morning, I dressed, got something to eat, and went to work. The incident was never mentioned again.

* * *

In September 1964, the high schools in the area participated in the round-robin games at the University of Tulsa. Our coaches at Tulsa's Memorial High School led the team to an undefeated season. In the playoffs, we were defeated by Rogers. All hope for a state championship was over. Memorial wound up third in the state for 4A football.

My first year out of high school, I played at Connors Junior College for Harold Cagle. The season wasn't kind to us, but I learned a lot.

During the last practice before our first game against Oklahoma Military Academy, I cracked my helmet. It took four stitches to close the hole in the top of my head. Coach Cagle told me I could suit up for the game, but he would not play me.

I kept bugging him along the sidelines until he finally let me go in for a kick-off. When the receiving team was going on the field, he nodded to me. That was to be my last play of the game.

My stepfather and mother were getting a divorce. It didn't affect me one way or the other, but Coach Cagle came by my dorm room several times just to talk. He always seemed to say the right thing. He wasn't only a good coach, he was a good man.

When the season was over, I got a job on weekends working at Brad's Gulf in Tulsa at 31st and Sheridan. Brad and his wife, Norma took me under their wings. They treated me like a son. We frequently did things together.

On the spur of the moment, Brad said, "Let's go get a *coney*."

The three of us piled into Brad's car and headed to downtown Tulsa to the Coney Island.

One weekend, we went to the Prison Rodeo in McAlester. Brad kept a few horses on land he leased by the airport. The three of us went out to fix fence.

Just as we were closing the station one night, Brad asked me, "Have you ever branded cattle?"

"No."

"You get here early tomorrow morning. A friend of mine at Big Cabin is going to do branding and needs help. About seven."

"I'll be here."

I had seen cattle being branded on TV and in the movies. It didn't strike me as being that hard to do. The next day, I learned just how tough it really was.

We got there about 8:30. The wranglers had around fifty head in one large pen. I helped run four head at a time into a chute with a gate at one end. We put a long piece of pipe behind the last animal. With all four pinned in the chute, I was told to reach in and grab on by the tail, twist it, and pull it tight against the fence.

One of the wranglers grabbed a hot branding iron and pressed it into the animal's flank. The smell of burning flesh was indescribable.

With a loud bellow, the steer sent a stream of shit to the ground— along the tail, and on my hands and leg. My gloves became slick, making it hard to hold the animals tight against the fence.

"Boy, hold that animal!"

That went on until the four steers were branded. They were released and four more were paraded into the chute. As I stood there ready to grab the next animal's tail, an old wrangler wearing an old beat-up straw cowboy hat and lipping a cigarette saw me staring at my gloves. Both were covered in cow shit.

As he talked, that cigarette moved up and down. "You know son, that's clean 'til it hits the ground."

Several years later, Norma died of brain cancer. At her funeral, I had tears in my eyes. I loved them both.

* * *

In January of 1966, I got my first car—a '55 Chevrolet convertible. It made me more independent. Between school and work, I spent very little time at home.

That summer, I went to work for Frank Neely Stone Company driving a truck and hauling rock out of quarries. When he was short of men, I did labor on the job sites.

I drove one truck. Dave Wadlow drove the other.

Dave was a big man, every bit of six feet tall and tipped the scales at 220 pounds. He had a barrel chest, thick legs, big arms, and a beard.

Down in the quarry there was no wind. The air was stale—especially busting up rocks with a ten- or twenty-pound sledgehammer. We hand-picked the rocks a mason would use on a new home. It was hard work.

Each truck could carry up to twenty-three tons. It was loaded by hand.

My weight stayed at 172 pounds. I was leaner and found muscles I didn't know I had. It crossed my mind to go back to school, but the thought didn't last long.

During that summer I began thinking about the Corps. I thought of doing three years of active duty, gain weight, mature and—at the end, have a better idea as to where my life was going.

There would be time to play ball again, but I had no idea how big of a change was coming.

2

MARINE CORPS RECRUIT DEPOT (MCRD)

*Most men lie about something, that they're
faster or stronger than other men.*

JOINING THE CORPS HAD BEEN on my mind for years. When I was twelve, a friend invited me to go on a short trip to the Port of Houston. A Navy cruiser came up the Houston ship channel from the Gulf and docked at the port. As the two of us explored the ship, we somehow wandered into an off-limits area. It wasn't long before a Marine in a blue uniform discovered us and chased us out.

I told my buddy, "Did you see that uniform? That was a Marine."

Over the years I watched movies about Marines, read *Battle Cry*, and knew someday I, too, would become a Marine.

During the summer of '66, I talked to a recruiter in Tulsa. His quota was full, but he said he would make some calls. He said maybe I could join in Arkansas.

A few days later, he called. I was to go to Ft. Smith. The recruiter there would sign me up.

It wasn't a bad drive from Tulsa. I signed the papers. On 8 October, I needed to be in Little Rock. There would be testing then. At some point, I would fly to San Diego, California.

The Corps had been on my mind for several years. It was time.

In Little Rock as I went through paperwork, I noticed a room off to my left. There were two young men seated at a table, with another man standing over them. When I asked one of the men in charge of our group what was going on, he told me the two men sitting down were being given their paperwork orally. They couldn't read.

My first night there, the government put me and the other young men up in a rather seedy hotel. The toilet and showers were down the hall. The hotel lights outside the window flashed on-and-off, reflecting off the wall and lulled me to sleep.

Our flight left the next day, just after dark. We would land in San Diego about four in the morning. It was my first time flying, so it seemed a little exciting.

Having no idea what to expect, I saw a Marine sergeant sitting a few rows in front of me. The seat next to him was empty. I decided to go forward and ask if I could sit with him for a moment.

"Do you mind if I sit down?"

"Not at all."

"I'm going to Marine boot camp. I was wondering if you could tell me what to expect."

He was blunt and to the point, "Do as you are told and keep your mouth shut."

It seemed like good advice. Excusing myself, I went back to my seat. Closing my eyes, I decided to take a nap. As my eyes closed, the thought crossed my mind, *What have you got yourself into this time, JB? I'll take whatever comes.*

I didn't realize it at the time, but I had been preparing for it my whole life.

When we finally landed in San Diego and as we were exiting the plane, a Marine sergeant said in a loud voice, "All you men who are here for Marine boot camp, line up over here."

After we lined up, he said, "There is a gray bus outside this door. When I give you the order, you will move out and get onto the bus. Move OUT! Move. Move. Move!"

We moved to the bus, found a seat, and waited for whatever was to come next.

The sergeant entered the bus. "You men are here to become United States Marines. You will each sit at attention, mouths shut, no looking around. Eyeballs straight ahead. All right driver, let's go."

We drove to the base, stopping at the main gate. I had been in the Corps for exactly thirty minutes.

The bus came to a halt inside the grounds.

The sergeant spoke up, "In a moment, I will tell you recruits to exit the bus. Outside, on the grinder you will find sets of yellow footprints. Find a pair and stand on them. NOW, move, move, move!"

We ran out of the bus, found footprints, and stood—waiting. A sign overhead, right in front of us, caught my attention.

To Be a Marine

You have to believe in Yourself

Your fellow Marine

Your Corps

Your Country

Your God.

Semper Fidelis

Like Grandma's night shirt, it covered everything.

After a few moments, they led us inside the building—one line at a time. First, we got haircuts. Then, we took off everything on our person to be mailed back home. From there, we were issued our first utilities, boots, and a cover (hat). Running back outside to the grinder (about ten acres of asphalt), we had our first greeting with our drill instructors.

"When I give you the command, you will step off on your left foot. We will march to our area. You will be assigned a bunk, a locker, a combination lock. Tomorrow, you will receive a second pair of boots, extra utilities, and gear for personal hygiene. Right now, you should have nothing on you that is of a personal nature. The Corps will provide for all your needs.

"Platoon 2238, right face, HUHH. Forward HUHH!"

Once we reached our area, the drill instructors assigned us to Quonset huts. We were told to find a bunk and get into it. When reveille sounded over the loudspeakers, we were to get dressed, square away our bunk, and be on the platoon street in formation before it stopped. He also reminded us the first word and the last word out of our sewers (mouths) was sir.

"It's either, 'Sir, yes sir,' or 'Sir, aye-aye, sir.' Do you ladies understand?"

Hollering from our bunks, "Sir, yes sir!"

"Goodnight, ladies."

"Sir, yes sir!"

I had barely closed my eyes when I heard, "Platoon 2238, on the platoon street."

We jumped out of bed, put on our utilities, laced up our boots, made our bunks, and tried to get out the door on time. Drill instructors were in each Quonset hut, yelling at the top of their lungs.

"Move private, move! You people are slow. But we can do better, can't we?!"

"Sir, yes sir!"

"I still can't hear you!"

"Sir, yes sir!"

"Now, when reveille is sounded in the morning, you will be dressed, have your bunk made, and be on the platoon street ready to march to chow, won't you?"

"Sir, yes sir!"

"I still can't hear you!"

"Sir, yes sir!"

"Platoon 2238, hit those racks!"

"Sir, yes sir!"

We ran to our bunks, broke down to our skivvies, and climbed into bed. I lay there for some time thinking the drill instructors would soon have us back on the platoon street.

My eyes got heavy. I fell asleep. The next thing I heard was reveille.

"Move, move! Platoon 2238, get on the platoon street. You people are slow. You're trying to upset me!"

"Sir, no sir!"

"You people are trying to make me look bad, aren't you?"

"Sir, no sir!"

"Platoon, forward, HUHH!"

As we moved to the chow hall, I'm sure everybody was thinking the same thing—we'll sit down, eat our breakfast, and have a few minutes to relax.

WRONG.

"You people will take a tray, slide your tray along—standing at attention. You will speak to no one. Once you have your food, you will sit down at attention. Once your table is full, I will give the order, 'Ready, eat.' You will not start eating until you are given the order. Do you people understand?"

"Sir, yes sir."

JB second from right in chow line.

We sat at attention until our table was full.

"Ready, eat!"

You could feel us begin to relax as we filled our forks. The drill instructors sensed it, too. I don't think I ate three bites when suddenly, "Get up and get out! Get out! Get out!"

We grabbed our trays. Walking by a trash can, we dumped our trays, laid the empty trays on a table, and hurried outside to get in formation.

After that first morning when we heard, "Ready, eat," forks and spoons banged against aluminum trays. Each of us shoveled food down our throats as fast as we could.

Those first few weeks were probably the hardest—getting the routine down, learning other's names, and where they were from.

Everyone was spoken to in the third person—the sergeant, the drill instructor, the private. If you went or were sent to the duty hut just across from our Quonset huts, you stood at attention, banged on the board next to the door—hitting it hard with your fist, and said, "Sir, the private requests permission to enter."

If there was no reply, you kept hitting the building until one of the drill instructors said, "Speak" or "Enter." It took a few days, but we got the regimen down.

At the end of the first week, the drill instructors picked four squad leaders. The young man who was picked for my squad told me he didn't want the job, so I took it. The drill instructors never said a word.

We were into our third week when my wisdom teeth gave me trouble. My back gums were swollen. It was hard to eat and sleep. I finally said something to Sgt. Dominguez.

"Sir, the private requests permission to speak to the drill instructor."

"Speak."

"Sir, the private is having a problem with his wisdom teeth."

"Open your mouth. ...Report back to me in thirty minutes."

"Sir, aye-aye sir!"

When I went back to the duty hut, the sergeant took me across the grinder to see a dentist. We entered the office. I was instructed to take a seat until I was called for. About ten minutes later, the dentist opened his door.

"In here, young man."

As I sat in his dental chair, he told me, "Relax and open your mouth wide. You've got quite an infection in both your lower wisdom teeth."

As he took a probe and stuck it in the back of my mouth, puss shot out and hit him on the mask he wore.

"That was quite painful, I'm sure. I'm going to give you a couple of shots so we can get this over with. You won't feel anything after it takes effect."

The dentist took out my wisdom teeth on both sides, putting a couple of stitches that would deteriorate over time.

The drill instructor and I left. We headed back to our area, and then to the obstacle course. The platoon was on the course for about two hours, then we got into formation and headed back to our area.

As we marched away, I had blood in my mouth, so I turned my head to the right and spit.

I suddenly heard, "Platoon, HALT! Redus! Front and center!"

I smartly made a right face and ran to the rear of the platoon. Staff Sergeant Phelps stood there. In the seconds it took me to cover the ground between us, quick thoughts ran through my head.

What does he want? Has someone in my squad fucked up?

My questions were going to be answered in just a few feet more. As I came to a stop about two feet from him, his large right hand reached out and wrapped around my throat. It was a little startling. I had just stopped and come to attention.

"Did you just spit a big green luncher out of my platoon?"

Trying to get the words out of my mouth wasn't easy. Air was hard to come by. My voice was labored.

"Sir, the private's mouth was bleeding, sir!"

"If I want any shit out of you, I'll unscrew the top of your head and dip it out. If you spit from my platoon again, you are going to be bleeding all over! Now disappear."

"Sir, aye-aye sir!"

Making an about-face, I returned to the platoon.

Staff Sgt Phelps was a big man, about six-feet two inches, 220 lbs. I swallowed any blood that accumulated in my mouth from then on.

That evening, some of the guys in my platoon were having a good time making sport of me. Just before taps, they took turns being Sgt Phelps while one of the other guys played me. We laughed so loud, I told them to hold it down. They were going to get Phelps in there.

"He'll call us out on the platoon street for PT."

* * *

On November 10, 1966, the Corps celebrated a birthday. While marching on the grinder, the Marine Corps Hymn was played over the loudspeakers. Everyone felt a little taller. Whether we were or not was not the point. We got it. The Marines who came before us left a legacy. The future was on our shoulders. We would not fail them.

Boot camp in the Corps was an experience that, on paper, did not give it justice. It's a time in a young man's life that had to be lived to be understood.

Ask any Marine about his time at MCRD or Paris Island. The Corps took a platoon of individuals and molded them into a unit that thought and acted as one. Blacks, Whites, Irish, and Italian heritage—pushed them, broke them down, built them up, and made them MARINES. It wasn't easy, pain was involved—physical and mental. But pain could be a great motivator.

Boot camp in the Corps usually lasted twelve weeks. But because of the war, it was cut back to nine weeks. About halfway through, the platoon left for Camp Pendleton to learn how to properly fire our weapon—the M-14.

We lived in barracks—a short march to Edson Range. The first few days were spent in classes, going over the nomenclature of the weapon, then snapping-in or dry firing.

During one of the classes, the platoon was seated in bleachers. The instructor was below us. I was in about the fifth row from the bottom.

I don't know if I hadn't gotten enough sleep the night before or if it was his voice. For whatever reason, my eyelids got real heavy. I rubbed my eyes, changed position, tried to stretch and rub my neck—anything I could do to stay awake.

Once, while rubbing my neck I noticed the instructor looking right at me. I stared back. A few minutes went by, and it started again. Trying to cover my mouth, I fought to keep my eyes open.

Not realizing I had closed my eyes, I woke myself up. Opening my eyes, all I saw was this Marine sergeant climbing up the bleachers, pushing men below me aside like a raging bull. He was on me in a matter of seconds.

"I'll teach you to sleep in my class." He grabbed me by my utility blouse. Hanging onto me, he dragged me down the bleachers. "Attention! You stand right here at the side of this table."

"Sir, aye-aye sir."

The M-14 had a hinge-butt plate on the end. Holding the weapon perpendicular, the butt on the table next to me, the barrel pointed towards the sky, the instructor said, "Put your shooting finger in the hinge-butt plate."

I put my right index finger between the hinge and the butt.

He grabbed the barrel in his right hand and pressed down.

It was like putting your finger in the hinge of a door and having someone slowly close the door with your finger in it.

He applied more pressure as I stood there. The other Marines definitely watched.

I gritted my teeth and stood there, trying to show no pain. I couldn't tell you what he said as we stood there. The pain was more than enough to deal with. Time seemed to drag on.

I don't know how long my finger was in that vice. The minutes dragged until he finally said the class was over—we needed to move to the next bleacher.

He turned, looked at me, raised the weapon releasing my finger, and walked off.

As I looked at my finger while walking to the next class, some of the Marines came up to me.

"Let's see your finger."

"I saw him watching you. The next thing I knew, he was climbing those bleachers flying to get to you."

"Who woulda thought? I have never seen anything like that. But, he must have done that before."

"Damn, my fucking finger is throbbing. Look. The nail is split."

"There's pink liquid running out from under. Your finger is flat, and it's got an impression on the bottom from the plate. Little squares."

"He knew exactly what he was doing. He has done this before."

"You said that already."

"Man, I don't know what happened. I just couldn't keep my eyes open. For some reason I just got sleepy."

As we marched to the next class, I thought it might be a good thing. I had heard one of the instructors say, "Bite down on your shooting finger. Make it sensitive. You're less likely to jerk the trigger."

The following day we were on the range—our first day of live fire. The Corps took marksmanship seriously.

"A Marine and his rifle is the most dangerous weapon in the world."

Our second day on the range, we moved from the 200-yard to the 300-yard firing line. The drill instructor with us was Sgt. Dominguez.

"I want all squad leaders over here. Now!"

The four of us gathered around him.

"Your men are not ready when they come up to the firing line. They don't have their slings ready. Their shooting gloves aren't on. They haven't changed their dope. Their record books aren't open and ready to write down their score. Fix it!"

"Sir, aye-aye sir."

I went back to the men in my squad. I watched each one and made sure they had their shit together.

When it came my turn to fire, I was in the prone position. I fired ten rounds from 300 yards. All ten rounds landed just below the target.

Just as I fired my last round, Sgt. Dominguez stood next to me. He hit me behind my right ear with a stick that had a large knot on one end.

"Private, do you know what this is?"

"Sir, yes sir. It's a do-right stick, sir."

"That's right private. And, what does this do-right stick do?"

"Sir, it makes you do right when you do wrong, sir."

"That's right, private. What did you do wrong?"

"Sir, the private forgot to change his dope from two hundred yards to three hundred yards, sir."

As he popped me a couple of times with the do-right stick behind my right ear, "Didn't I just tell you and the other squad leaders to get your men ready for the firing line? And didn't that include you?"

Sir, yes sir."

"It's just a thought, but you might want to fix that," he got in my face, "before you fire off-hand."

"Sir, yes sir."

We finished firing for the day and headed back to the barracks. Sitting outside on our buckets, we cleaned our weapons. Sgt Dominguez, who was sitting on the steps to the barracks, spoke up.

"Where's the private who forgot his dope on his weapon today?"

I immediately stood up. "Sir, Private Redus, sir."

"Front and center, Turd. Get over here."

I laid my weapon down on the asphalt and ran to the stairs where Sgt Dominguez sat, below the door to the barracks. I stood at attention.

"You're a squad leader, aren't you, Redus?"

"Sir, yes sir."

"Do you think squad leaders should be treated better than anyone else?"

"Sir, no sir. They should be treated worse, sir."

"Meet me in the head tonight when the lights go out."

"Sir, yes sir."

"Now, get out of my sight."

I took one step back and said, "Sir, aye-aye sir."

That night at 2100, the lights were turned off. Taps was being played through the base loudspeaker. I went to the head, located on one end of the barracks.

The light was on in the head. Sgt Dominguez was waiting.

"Take off your t-shirt and dog tags. Place them in the sink."

"Sir, aye-aye sir."

When I had done what he said, I returned and stood at attention, wearing only my skivvies and shower shoes.

"I told you to square your men away at the range today didn't I, private?"

"Sir, yes sir."

But you, private, chose to go to the firing line unprepared."

"Sir, yes sir."

Just as the words left my mouth, he turned and hit me in the stomach. I saw the blow coming and tightened my stomach.

He walked back-and-forth, telling me again how I had defied his order. Standing in front of me, his right arm moved. I tightened up just as the blow hit my stomach.

"Don't tighten up. Don't tighten up!"

"Sir, yes sir."

It was between me and the sergeant. He wanted me to go to my knees. But I had decided no matter how many times he hit me, I was not going down.

Time seemed to drag on.

He punched me in the stomach and then yelled in my face, "Don't you tighten up on me."

My response was always the same, "Sir, yes sir."

I don't know how many times he punched me, but later a tear came out of my right eye and rolled down my cheek. He must have seen it. He told me to gather my gear and hit the rack.

As I headed to my bunk, several of the other recruits gathered around me.

"We all saw what he did."

"Let's go in there and grab that son-of-a-bitch and beat the shit out of him."

"No, let it go. Let it go. Get in your bunks."

There was grumbling, but they went to their bunks. My stomach was sore. Before I knew it though, I, too, was asleep.

The next morning as reveille blew, I got up and headed for the head to shave and brush my teeth. My stomach was sore. I rubbed my belly.

Lifting up my t-shirt, I saw my stomach was black and blue with a little green and yellow. From nipple to nipple and down to my belly button, the bruises formed a square on my chest.

Finishing in the head, I got dressed, grabbed my weapon, and went outside for formation. The platoon marched to the range.

JB on the left preparing for dry firing.

I never forgot to put my dope on my weapon again. If I had made that mistake on qualification day, I would not have qualified and lost my job as squad leader—and the stripe that came with it.

With only a few more days to go at the range, we headed back to the barracks. As we stood in formation, Staff Sgt Phelps came up to me.

"Redus, you've got a man out of line. Square him away."

As I leaned out looking down the line, Nicky stuck out from the rest of the squad. I walked down the line of recruits until I stood in front of him.

"DiMaggio, move back." With my right hand, I backhanded him across his face.

He looked at me and gritted his teeth. "I'm gonna kill you. I'm gonna kill you!"

He moved back into position. I returned to the head of the squad. We put our weapons in the barracks and marched off to chow.

Nicky was Italian—hot tempered and tough. I knew at some point we would have to settle it.

During chow, I got up and went over to the milk dispenser. The next thing I knew, Nicky was standing beside me.

He said just one word, "Outside."

"I'll be right there, Nicky."

As I walked down the steps, Nicky stood about twenty feet away. It was dark outside. We would settle it away from the lights.

Not a word was spoken between us. We both knew why we were there.

As we stood there with our hands up, Sgt Parker came out of nowhere. We both jumped to attention.

"What are you two turds doing?" Facing Nicky, he yelled, "Are you fucking with one of my squad leaders? Both of you get to the duty hut."

Neither of us said a word. Once in the duty hut, we stood next to each other at attention. Sgt Parker stood there in front of us, hollering at Nicky.

"You want to fuck with one of my squad leaders, then you fuck with me."

He suddenly hit Nicky with a right cross, and Nicky went down.

Standing at attention, I could barely see Nicky. He wasn't moving. My first thought was, *I'm next.*

The sergeant moved in front of me.

"Get this thing out of my duty hut."

"Sir, yes sir."

As I moved to pick up Nicky, another Marine moved toward us.

"I've got him. I've got him."

I picked up Nicky. I put him over my shoulder and walked to the head.

Laying him down on the deck, I took off my blouse and wadded it up, forming a pillow to put under his head. He was out cold.

"Nicky, I'm sorry man. I never meant for this to happen."

Turning on a faucet, I cupped my hands—filling them with water. Splashing the water in his face several times, he came around.

"Nicky, Nicky! I'm sorry man."

With his eyes open, he looked up at me, shook his head, and stuck out his hand.

"Help me up."

I grabbed his hand and arm, lifting him up.

"Boy, that jack-off knocked my dick stiff!"

"After he hit you, I thought I was next. But he just told me to get you outta there."

"I don't remember anything. The last thing I do remember was him hollering, then I came to on the floor with you standing over me."

"Come on, Nicky. Let's go outside and get some air."

Outside, we shook hands. It never came up again. I still believe the drill instructors watched Nicky and me. They knew a fight was inevitable, and it would be bloody.

With the qualifications over and the range behind us, we loaded onto a bus and returned to MCRD.

* * *

Every platoon did a week of KP duty, except for the guide and squad leaders. The five of us were sent across the grinder to hand-deliver messages between the officers who ran the base.

Sergeant Dominguez put me outside the colonel's office and told me not to move. He said he would be right back. A few minutes passed. A Marine captain came up to me.

"Come with me, recruit."

"Sir, my drill instructor told me to stand right here, not to move, sir."

"Now I'm telling you to come with me. Your drill instructor will understand. The colonel wants to have a word with you."

"Sir, yes sir."

As I entered the colonel's office, he was seated at his desk.

"Come in, recruit. Stand over here, at ease."

"Sir, yes sir."

"What week are you in recruit?"

"Sir, the private is in his seventh week, sir."

"What's the most important thing you've learned so far?"

"Sir, discipline. It will save my life in combat, sir."

"Private, have you been abused at any time since you've been here?"

"Sir, no sir."

I wasn't aware of it at the time, though I did hear the door open and close behind me—Sergeant Dominguez had come into the room right after I did.

"Alright, private, I think that's all I need. You can return to your platoon."

I took one step back. "Sir, aye-aye sir."

Doing an about-face, I noticed Sgt Dominguez standing by the door. He and I walked back across the grinder, back to our area. Not a word was spoken.

The next week, the platoon got back together. They were done with KP, and squad leaders were through running messages.

Pugil sticks—an aggressive way of training to learn how to use a bayonet without sticking anyone—were used to just club 'em to death.

The pit was about forty feet across, making a large circle. There was a sandbag at two points. The two men who fought each other stood on the sandbags until the instructor blew a whistle. One man charged the other and fought until the instructor blew his whistle again—the signal to stop.

The pugil stick was about four feet long, with padding on either end. Both men wore a football helmet and protective gloves. During boot camp we worked on that exercise two to three times a week.

One day another platoon had made a challenge. They wanted our platoon to send out our best man, meet in the circle, and fight it out with their best man.

Upon hearing that information from Sgt Dominguez, the platoon immediately yelled and hollered, "DiMaggio, DiMaggio."

I hollered, "DiMaggio, DiMaggio."

The other platoon hollered for their man.

We were excited. Nicky was tough. He would beat the hell out of their man.

During the excitement, Sgt Dominguez came over to me, grabbed me by the arm, took me aside, and whispered in my ear.

"Redus, you're going to fight for us. If you don't win, you and I are going back into the head tonight."

"Sir, yes sir."

Dominguez hollered out and the platoon quieted down.

"Is your man ready?"

Dominguez had his hand on my shoulder. "Right here. We're ready. This is our man."

As I stood on the sandbag waiting for the instructor's whistle, my adrenaline was pumping. The instructor blew his whistle.

I charged toward the other recruit, running as hard as I could across the sand. With the pugil stick firmly in my hands, I didn't wait for my opponent in the center. It was serious for me. Bringing my stick up to port, just before I got to him, I used it like a bayonet.

Using my momentum, the end of the pugil caught him by the throat. His head snapped backward. His feet went up in the air about as high as my shoulders. He landed on his back. I stabbed him in the chest, his crotch, and launched a butt stroke to his head.

At the moment the other recruit hit the ground, the instructor hollered at me, "Kill him, Kill him!"

The platoon went wild.

A whistle was blown, and it was over.

My whole platoon ran over, screaming and yelling.

I saw Dominguez look at me. He had a big smile on his face. That was the only time I ever saw him smile.

Grabbing Nicky by the arm, I said, "You would have done just as well."

Nicky was a tough kid.

* * *

Graduation was a few days away. There was talk that once we got to Pendleton for infantry training, we might go home for Christmas.

At night if I stood at the end of our platoon street, I saw Christmas lights flickering in the distant San Diego.

The following day, we were to march over to the tailor shop and pick up our uniforms. As taps came over the loudspeaker, I laid in my bunk thinking how much we had changed—what we had been through together.

My eyes were heavy. I needed sleep.

With graduation looming, Sgt Dominguez marched us over to the photography hut to pick up our platoon photo. Each of us would receive one.

I was sure as years passed, it would be looked at from time-to-time—a chance to remember.

The sergeant walked out of the building, toward us with a swift gate. From the look on his face, something was not right.

He passed by me with the photos under one arm, except for one in his right hand.

"Private, look at this photo. Look at it. Just before the photographer snapped his camera, I told all of you to have the look of a natural-born killer. A natural-born killer, private. A natural-born killer! Look at your face! You're smiling, private! You don't look like a killer. There're no do-overs, private. Every man in this platoon looks like a killer—a killer, except for you!"

"Sir, yes sir."

"We're gonna double-time it back to our area. Platoon, Attention! Platoon right turn. Huhh! Platoon, double time. Huhh!"

We ran all the way back to our platoon street.

Once there, Sgt Dominguez called a halt. With us standing at attention, he passed out the photos.

"Platoon dismissed."

As we headed for our Quonset huts, every man opened his folder. Sure enough, there was Taylor—grinning from ear-to-ear. Everyone else had the look of a natural-born killer.

* * *

Graduation day, out in front of the theatre at one end of the grinder, General B. A. Hockmuth said a few words about the Corps and the legacy we had inherited. Staff Sergeant Phelps stood at the top of the stairs.

"Platoon 2238, fall out."

Up in the air went our covers. Shaking hands, slapping backs, congratulating each other—we had made it.

Sgt Dominguez came over to me and shook my hand.

"Congratulations, Marine."

"Thank you, sir."

As he walked away I thought to myself, *I'm never going to forget him. You know, he looks a lot like Jack Webb.*

The next day, we left for Camp Pendleton. The platoon had gathered in one Quonset hut to hear Staff Sergeant Phelps read off each man's MOS.

Most of us figured we would be sent to the grunts, get more training, then leave for Vietnam. As it turned out, most of us were going to the infantry, except for a couple Marines sent to drive trucks.

When my name was called, the sergeant said, "Redus 0300, Sea School."

I wasn't quite sure what that meant, Sea School.

What is that?

Speaking to one of the sergeants, I was informed it was where they teach you about the Navy. Marines were attached to fighting ships to provide security. It had been that way for almost 200 years.

After infantry training, I was to report back to MCRD. Sea School was on the opposite end of the grinder from the auditorium.

"There's a big sign. You can't miss it," someone told me.

For once, the rumor was true. We were going home for Christmas. They were going to turn us loose on the 23rd of December. We would get two weeks then report back to Camp Pendleton for infantry training.

Loading buses, duffel bags in hand, we headed for the LA airport.

The airport was crowded as I made my way to Delta Airlines. I hadn't given much thought until then about people traveling for the holidays. It was my first time to fly military standby. I didn't have much cash. Surely, I wouldn't have a long wait.

As the hours went by, I checked with the airlines. Still no seat. Late into the night, I sat on a couch with my duffel bag between my legs and fell asleep.

I woke up the next morning to the sound of a vacuum cleaner being pushed along the carpet in front of me.

Standing up, I stretched and then went to the head to wash the sleep out of my eyes. I made another trip to the airline counter but still no seat.

It was the morning of the 24th—I wasn't sure if I would get a flight that day.

Maybe I should think about the train or take a bus. There was a small restaurant nearby. *Coffee and a donut...* I would figure it out.

As I sat there sipping my coffee and eating my donut, two ladies sat near me.

"Going home for Christmas?

"Well, I'm not sure. I am flying military stand-by, but so far I haven't had much luck. I hadn't given much thought to all these people trying to get home, too. I'm thinking about cashing in my ticket and taking a bus or train. Then I'll have money to eat on. It'll take me a couple of days to get home, but eventually I'll get there."

"Where are you from?"

"Oklahoma." I sat there, drinking my coffee.

The two ladies got up. "When you finish your coffee, come by our ticket counter, just out the door and to your left. There may be something we can do. By the way, which airlines are you flying?"

"Delta."

"You come and see us."

"Yes ma'am."

I finished my coffee, grabbed my duffel bag, and headed out the door.

Her ticket counter was familiar to me. I had stopped by there several times since the day before. There probably wasn't much she could do, but what could it hurt to try?

I didn't see her right off but suddenly there she was, coming out of a back room.

"Ma'am?"

"Yes, hello. Let me see your ticket. I'll be right back."

She was gone for five or ten minutes then appeared again with a big smile on her face.

"Merry Christmas, Marine."

She handed me the ticket. I opened it, hardly believing my eyes. It was a complete ticket, no stand-by.

"Ma'am, this is a complete ticket. I don't know what to say."

"You don't have to say anything. You better hurry. Your flight is getting ready to take passengers."

"Thank you, ma'am. Thank you. Merry Christmas."

I grabbed my duffel bag and headed for the gate.

I wouldn't recognize that lady if she walked up to me, but I remembered it as the kindest thing anyone has ever done for me. I knew her for just a few minutes. I was nothing to her, but I remember her in my prayers.

It was Christmas Eve, 1966.

3

SEA SCHOOL; USS *ST PAUL*; USS *NEWPORT NEWS*

"What is life without a little diversion?" ~ Paths of Glory

AFTER I FINISHED REGIMENTAL INFANTRY training at Camp Pendleton, I loaded on a bus and went back to MCRD and Sea School. My class had thirty Marines and two NCOS. The school lasted about a month. We were taught how to wear the dress blues we were issued. We were trained in Naval history and Naval slang. We learned *port* from *starboard*, the *deck, bow* to *stern*, a *hatch, dogging wrenches*, etc.

Being able to recognize the rank of Naval officers and Navy personal was included in our training. We were given tests and grades were taken. The NCOs showed us how to get our shoes and the bill of our covers to shine like patent leather.

There were a lot of inspections of not only our lockers and personal gear, but also our brass and the creases in our blouse. We wore the uniform every day.

Before our test scores were put on the bulletin board, we would be interviewed by the colonel. I was a little nervous, but I felt I had done my best. When my turn came, I knocked on the colonel's hatch.

"Enter."

I walked into the colonel's office and stood about two feet from his desk at attention.

"Sir, PFC Redus."

"Stand at ease, Marine."

"Yes sir."

He asked me a few questions, which I thought I answered well.

Then he said, "Do you have any idea what this piece of paper I'm holding in my hand says?"

"No sir."

"It's a handwritten note from your sergeant. Would you like for me to read it to you?"

Several things were going through my head at that moment. *I can't say no. Just read the damn note. I'll take whatever comes.*

"Yes sir."

"Your sergeant has written here, 'I wish I had twenty more just like him'. Now, lance corporal, what do you think about that?"

"Sir, I don't know what to say. Sir, did the colonel just say 'lance corporal'?"

He pushed his chair back and stood up. "The increase in rank is a result of you graduating at the head of your class."

"Sir, this is a bit of a surprise. I had no idea."

He stuck out his hand. "That sergeant of yours is a very demanding Marine. You obviously worked very hard. He apparently took note."

"Sir, aye-aye sir."

I left the building, walked outside, and stared across the grinder. My old platoon street, along with the row of Quonset huts were about 200 yards away.

It started there about five months prior. According to my orders, I was to leave the next day for Long Beach. I was to be a Flag Marine for Admiral Walter Vincent Combs, Commander of ComCruDesFlot 3.

* * *

I took a cab from the bus station. I arrived at the naval base in Long Beach about one o'clock in the morning. Showing my orders to a Navy chief, he told me to have a seat. He would make a call. Someone would come to pick me up.

"Would you like a cup of coffee?"

"Thanks, Chief."

It didn't take long for a Marine to pull up in a shiny black car.

"My name's JT. I'm the one on duty aboard ship tonight. One of us has to be on board every night in case the admiral gets an important message. He and his wife live here on the base, so if he gets a message at three o'clock in the morning, whoever is on duty jumps in the car and takes it to him. Is that your gear?"

"You bet."

He grabbed my duffel bag, threw it into the back seat, and off we went.

"What ship are we on?"

"The *Bryce Canyon*, it's a destroyer tender. The destroyers moor up alongside the *Canyon*. The sailors on the *Canyon* can fix anything."

"What's the admiral like?"

"Well, he's a rear admiral, two stars, and he was on a destroyer in WWII. He's about medium height with gray hair. He loves boxing and likes to work a speed bag. We have five Marines on the staff.

A driver for the admiral and one for his chief of staff. There's three of us on duty every day during the week. The other two have the day off. We rotate shifts. It's on a paper tacked to a bulletin board on the bulkhead just outside our office."

We pulled up on the dock next to the *Bryce Canyon*. JT grabbed my gear and the two of us went aboard.

I got a little sleep in a bunk just inside the hatch of the Marine office. That morning at about 0800, I met the admiral, chief of staff, flag lieutenant, and two other Marines. They had been shorthanded, so they were glad to see me.

It took about two more weeks before the fifth Marine showed up. The staff was complete. It wouldn't be long before we would be flying to Subic Bay in the Philippines to board the admiral's flag ship, the USS *St Paul*.

Aboard the *St Paul*, it would be my first overseas trip. The flight took seventeen hours. We flew from California to Alaska, refueled, then flew on to Okinawa, and finally Clarke Air Base in the Philippines. The admiral's staff loaded into buses for the ride to Subic Bay Naval Base.

I was tired, and my feet were swollen. We were told not to take off our shoes during the flight, just to loosen the shoestrings. If we took off our shoes, our feet would swell from being in the air so long. There would be a problem getting our feet back in our shoes.

As we cleared the main gate, a few moments passed and there she was—the *St Paul*. I hadn't been aboard a cruiser since I was twelve years old. The *Paul* was lit up like a Christmas tree. I saw men working on her. Sparks flew from welding torches. She had three barrels on each turret of eight-inch guns, two forward and one aft. She was impressive.

We unloaded our gear and were led to our bunks. It took a few days to familiarize myself with the ship. By the second day, we left

Subic Bay and headed for the Gulf of Tonkin and the 7th Fleet Yacht Club. For the most part the *Paul* spent her time up north above the DMZ (demilitarized zone) firing at H&I (harassment and interdiction) targets, looking for WBLC (waterborne logistic craft). At times we fired in support of the Marines below the DMZ.

When the *Paul* went on a firing mission, if I wasn't on duty with the admiral or working in his fire control room, I found a spot in the middle of the ship above the water line.

Just before the *Paul's* big guns fired, a buzzer went off throughout the ship preparing everyone on board for the loud boom that was coming. We always had two destroyers with us on each fire mission. All three turned at the same time to either the port or starboard and fired several broadsides.

JB and Dan in front of the 8-inch gun mount. This was the summer of 1967 off the coast of North Vietnam.

When the order was given to turn and head back out to sea, I could tell when the ship suddenly picked up speed. You felt it in the way she moved, depending on where you were on the ship. You heard her engine whine louder and louder.

Sometimes the admiral went outside during a mission.

"Let's go outside, Redus."

"Aye-aye, sir."

I opened the metal hatch and led him outside onto a walkway. The eight-inchers went off, and I saw fire off the end of the barrel.

At night it was loud. The worse part was the soot that came out of the barrels. If the wind was blowing our way, it got in my eyes and mouth. One night, the admiral and I had just stepped outside during a mission. The *Paul*'s guns fired and the North Vietnamese coast suddenly lit up with one flash after another.

The admiral hollered, "Let's get out of here, Redus."

He beat me to the hatch. The NVA were apparently waiting for us. They had moved in more shore batteries that lit up the coastline. Neither the *Paul* or the two destroyers took a hit.

I especially liked going outside with the admiral during daylight hours. The shore batteries shot back at us.

In July 1967, the *St Paul* got a distress signal. The carrier *Forestall* was off the coast of North Vietnam. It was on fire. The *Paul* raced to the carrier's aid. It was a bright day with low swells. We approached her, keeping about two hundred yards between us. It was an incredible sight. The fantail was crumbled and bent like giant hand-kneaded dough. We stayed on station for several hours but there wasn't much we could do. The fire was under control, so the *Paul* left to go back online in the Tonkin Gulf.

Weeks later while at Subic Bay, I heard stories about sailors trapped below deck on the *Forestall*. The watertight doors had been shut to protect the ship. The sailors below had beat on the doors, hollering at the men outside to open them. Under direct order, the doors were not opened until it was determined the *Forestall* was not in danger of sinking. On the *Paul* when I wasn't on duty, I stayed in an area well above the waterline during a firing mission.

Months later Mr. Yonkers, our flag lieutenant told me what had happened aboard the *Forestall*. A jet on the flight deck had an accidental missile firing. The missile flew across the deck, hitting an A-4 Skyhawk in the fuel tank and caused a chain-reaction. Other planes nearby caught fire.

In 1970, I learned the pilot in the A-4 Skyhawk who took the missile in the fuel tank was John McCain. He suffered shrapnel wounds to his chests and legs. He returned to duty in 1968 to fly off the carrier *Oriskany* in the waters off North Vietnam.

JB in front of the Marine 5-inch gun mount on the St. Paul.

As the admiral and I stood outside hanging onto the railing, the *Paul* and her two destroyers headed back out to sea at full throttle. Artillery rounds hit the water, sending huge geysers—some as high as the top of the destroyers. It looked like a scene from an old World War II movie. If just one of those rounds had hit the ship in a crucial spot, it meant death or the crippling of the *Paul*. The NVA would find their range and pour it on.

One afternoon in early August 1967, we were on a firing mission up north. The *Paul* took a round up forward on the starboard side, about eight- to ten-feet above the waterline. No one was in any of the compartments at the time, so we had no injuries.

Out at sea, the damage was assessed. A decision was made. The *Paul* would return to the area where the shore batteries had fired on us and destroy them. After the mission, we headed for Subic Bay in the Philippines and got the needed repairs for the large hole in *Paul's* starboard side. Most everyone was a little disappointed. If we hadn't taken that hit, the ship was scheduled to go to Taiwan for a few days for shore leave.

The St. Paul *taking a hit while under fire in the Gulf of Tonkin*

Just outside of Subic was a small town called Olongapo, the armpit of the Pacific—a real shithole. There was a small bridge over a creek that you walked over to get there. As you walked the bridge, there were a few small boats with a pretty girl and a couple of boys waving and hollering, "Maline. Maline. Sailor boy. Sailor boy."

They wanted you to throw them a coin. If the girl couldn't catch the coin, one of the young boys dove into the water and grabbed the coin before it sank to the bottom.

I had seen Sailors and Marines intentionally throw coins in the creek, away from the girls. The water was dirty. It had raw sewage in it from the hooches hanging over the creek. There was very little light except for a few torches on the bridge. I never saw those boys fail to find a coin once it had hit the water.

Some of the streets had a little asphalt, but for the most part, the streets were dirt. Bars with names like TEXAS CLUB or the NEW YORK CLUB lined the streets on both sides. There was plenty of liquor and women.

Little kids came up to the men, "Do you want to fuck my mother? She is a virgin," or "Do you want short time or long time?"

Jitneys roamed the streets, picking up Sailors and Marines to take them to bars further down the street, or to bring them back to the bridge to stumble back to their barracks or ship. Young boys worked the street on both sides, selling cooked monkey meat in small chunks on a spit of bamboo.

I could get a facial for fifty cents and a rub-down for a quarter on the base. Most of the time I went to the gym, had a good work-out, a steam bath, a shower, and headed back to the ship for chow.

Danny, one of the flag Marines showed me a flyer. Some of the men from the Marine detachment were going to spend three days at a Jungle Survival Course. All we had to do was clear it through the flag lieutenant.

"It'll be great man. Three days in the jungle and learning how to survive. All we take with us is a knife and a sock to hold a handful of rice."

"I'm in. What about the other guys? Somebody's got to stay here on duty?"

"They're not interested. It's just you and me."

"We'll have to go into Olongapo and buy us a bolo?"

"Right, they're only a couple of bucks. Somebody told me they melt down old car springs to make them."

Danny and I went into town and bought our knives. The next day we were sitting in bleachers. Class had started.

The instructor told us all birds are edible. He then passed around a metal plate of cooked monkey meat and snake. Nobody wanted to act squeamish, so we took some of each from the plate. It wasn't bad. It was a little tough, but not bad.

Each group would have two *Negritos* as instructors. During World War II, the Japanese were scared to death of them. They would sneak into the enemy's camp at night, cut the throat of a sentry, and leave him sitting there as if he were asleep. Without disturbing the Japanese, the *Negritos* had infiltrated their camp. It worked hard on the nerves of the Japanese.

The Philippine bushmen—the *Negritos* were little people but very capable. Their English was almost nonexistent. My Filipino language skills were limited but somehow they taught us how to catch small fish and animals. Mixing what we caught with a little rice, they taught us how to cook using a section of bamboo and a little water and covering it with coals from the fire. It acted like a small pressure cooker. They showed us how to build our shelters off the ground with a small roof overhead using large leaves to hold back the rain.

Being in the jungle with the Negritos was one of the best experiences I had on my tour. After it was over, I shook their hands, bowed, and thanked them. The Japanese were correct in fearing them.

We were leaving early the following morning—going back on the line, back into the Gulf. The word was Marines were going to need the *St Paul* for fire support below the DMZ.

Once at sea, I liked spending time on the focsle, leaning over the bow as the *Paul* cut its way through the Gulf. As the wind and a light spray hit my face, dolphins off the starboard side raced the ship. Flying fish took to the air.

JB aboard the USS St Paul

Earlier in the day, a sailor pointed out a water spout in the distance. It reminded me of the tornadoes back in Oklahoma. The open ocean, sometimes like a sheet of glass would, within hours, changed to large swells with huge thunderheads in the distance—so beautiful.

We got caught in a typhoon once for about four days. Over the ship's loudspeaker came, "Now hear this, all hatches that go outside of the ship are to be closed and dogged down. No one is to go outside."

I knew of a hatch topside that had plenty of railing outside. When I was sure no one was watching, I quickly opened the hatch and stepped outside. The rain pelted me. The wind was incredible. As I stood there watching the *Paul* maneuver through the huge waves, the bow dipped into the ocean, covering the forecastle in salt water. It was incredible—the power of the ocean was being thrown at the big cruiser. I had to see it for myself not just sitting inside trying to imagine what was going on outside.

Once the typhoon was behind us, we headed back to the Gulf of Tonkin. The captain relayed a message to the admiral that a fighter jet caught a WBLC trying to make a run across the Gulf. The craft was carrying supplies from Hainan Island (which is Chinese) to Haipon Harbor. After blowing it up, the jet reported several survivors and debris in the water. The *St Paul* investigated.

As the ship pulled up next to the debris, four North Vietnamese were still alive—wearing yellow life jackets. A whaleboat was put over the side with four Marines from the detachment along for security. I leaned against the railing on the starboard side. Just as the whaleboat entered the debris field to pick up the survivors, someone yelled, "Shark!"

I looked at all four Vietnamese. As I watched, the man who was furthest from the boat suddenly disappeared. A shark had taken him down with a slap of his tail. The other three survivors swam toward the whaleboat as quickly as they could. After the survivors got aboard, the rescuer brought them to the ship. Several had shrapnel wounds in their arms and received medical treatment. All three were given clean clothes and placed in the brig.

As the *Paul* moved away, the fourth North Vietnamese who had been attacked by the shark floated by, face down. His right leg was gone.

The ship made her way to Da Nang where the prisoners were to be turned over to the Marines. A landing craft pulled alongside, as a rope ladder was tossed to the men below. The NVA were made to understand they were to climb down the side to the waiting boat. About halfway down they stopped. One of the Marines climbed up the rope ladder, grabbed the NVA, pried his hands off the rope, and made him fall the rest of the way. When the other two prisoners saw what happened, they screamed and yelled. They didn't want to go any further. The Marine again pried one, then the other off the ladder and they fell to the landing craft.

A Navy officer hollered at the Marines to be more careful with the prisoners, but it fell on deaf ears.

Then, the Marines tied the NVA's hands behind their backs, put burlap bags over their heads, and yelled at the boatswain's mate to head for the dock. For several days, it was the talk all over the ship the way the Marines had handled the prisoners. They didn't understand the war being fought aboard the ship was different than the war being fought in the jungles, mountains, and rice paddies of Vietnam.

Dan and JB off the coast of South Vietnam
aboard the USS St Paul *29 June 1967*

About five weeks went by before we had our first real liberty in a foreign port. Singapore sounded exciting. It would be great to walk the streets, check out the bars and eat their food.

Danny and I left the base and went into the city together. We hadn't gone far when we decided to get something to eat. Seeing what looked like a street vendor with a baker tent, he waved us over. Under a tarp, he had a large spool (like the ones they use in high power line wire) and two raised chairs. The waiter wore a turban. The menu was handwritten on a piece of paper. I ordered a chicken sandwich. Danny ordered a beef sandwich. As we sat there absorbing the culture, I looked around and there across the street was the biggest yellow cat I had ever seen.

"Danny, look at that."

"What?"

"That cat. Look, I think both his front paws are broken."

As the cat moved along the edge of a small building, just twenty feet from us, his front paws flopped up and down.

"Look at the head on that SOB. He swings it back and forth like he is looking for something."

Just as the cat disappeared from view, our waiter in the turban appeared with my chicken sandwich and a bottle of coke. He looked at Danny and said, "Your beef sandwich will be ready very soon."

As our waiter turned to go back in the tent, we heard a cat screaming and fighting behind the tent. Then, as suddenly as it started, it got quiet.

"Danny, they killed that cat. They're going to skin it and cook it. That cat is going to be your beef sandwich."

"No, they wouldn't do that."

"I'm telling you man, they saw that cat coming. They lured it in behind the tent and killed it."

Several minutes later our man reappeared with a big smile. He handed Danny his beef sandwich and a drink. He bowed and returned to the tent.

"I'm telling you, Danny. You're eating that cat."

"Just shut up and eat."

After eating we made our way down the street to find a watering hole. Checking the alleys along the street, we never saw that cat again.

Three days and two nights later, the *St Paul* left Singapore and headed out to sea. We were going to "Cross the Line"—the equator.

A ceremony, a great Navy tradition was going to take place. Once the exact position was reached, the ship slowed down. Navy chiefs dressed up like pirates, and the initiation began. To become a 'Shellback' you had to run a gauntlet on your hands and knees. At the end of that, you had to kiss King Neptune's belly button. King Neptune was usually the fattest sailor they could find. Then, you had to dive into a large tank full of trash and garbage and swim underwater to the other end, where a fire hose washed you off.

Marines from the detachment ran the gauntlet before the flag Marines. They saved the four of us for last. Just before it was my turn, I looked toward the back of the ship. There were over 1500 men on the *Paul*. It looked like most of them were there holding belts and sticks. The gauntlet snaked back and forth on the fantail.

They yelled, "Come on, Marine. Come on!"

I was told whatever you do, don't stop or they will beat you to death. They were not supposed to hit you on the head, but the chief said there were no promises.

Taking off on my hands and knees, I was told to get through the gauntlet as quickly as possible. On the other end, King Neptune was seated. He said a few words as he motioned me to drop to my knees. The he grabbed the back of my head and buried it in his belly, which was covered with lard.

When King Neptune finally released me, I moved to the large tank full of water and trash. The trash was from the leftover food from the past week plus whatever else they could find. I jumped in and swam underwater to the other end. I got out and a fire hose washed me off, front and back.

Danny waited for me and as we turned to walk away, a Navy chief came up behind me and put me in a chokehold and took me to the deck. The chief thought it was part of the game.

After the chief released me, Danny and I started to walk off. Danny asked, "You going to let him get away with that?"

"Nope." I turned, and headed back toward the chief.

"Oh, you want more, do you?"

As I closed the distance between us, he reached out to grab me. I grabbed him by the shoulders and swept his feet out from underneath him. He fell, and I grabbed him by the throat, digging my fingers into his windpipe. He hit the deck hard as I held onto his throat. I saw he was gasping for breath, when another Navy chief suddenly came up and hollered at me to let him go.

"That's an order, Marine. Let him go!"

I released my grip and got to my feet. The chief rolled over on the deck on his knees, spitting and coughing.

"I hope there are no hard feelings," I said.

The chief never said a word and I walked away.

Danny and I headed for the showers. For a while, I thought there might be blowback over the incident but nothing was ever said.

Becoming a Shellback was an honorable and colorful tradition—part of Naval tradition for well-over a hundred years. If you weren't a Shellback, you were a Pollywog.

In late August 1967, the admiral changed his flagship from the *St Paul* to the *Newport News*. At first, the staff were told both cruisers would dock in Da Nang Harbor. The admiral decided the exchange would take place at sea. With the two cruisers just sixty to eighty yards from each other, a line was sent over with a bigger line attached to it. As the two cruisers cut through the water, parallel to each other, we were to sit in a chair. We were each transferred to the

Newport News. I sat in the chair, hanging on about forty feet above the water. It was an incredible sight to sit in that chair as sailors on the *Paul* released line and sailors on the *Newport News* pulled each one of us across. What a sight it was, seeing the *Paul* on my left and the *News* to my right.

Several months before, the captain of the USS *Boston* had pulled up alongside the *Paul* to have a talk with the admiral. He was going back to his ship in the chair when the rope snapped. The chair fell into the water about halfway between both ships. A destroyer was following behind us. They picked up the captain.

It was a good thing he fell between the two cruisers. If he had fallen closer to either ship, he might have been sucked in the ship's current and pulled under into the screws. Needless to say, the admiral was not happy. The captain of the *Boston* was eventually returned to his ship.

I thought about the captain of the *Boston* falling into the water but only for a moment. Others had gone across before me. I would make it, too.

It was nice aboard the *News*. For one thing, it had air conditioning. On hot nights aboard the *Paul* when we were out at sea, I grabbed a life jacket and slept outside on the deck under the eight-inch turrets. The food was good on both ships. The Navy had great cooks.

The following day we got off the line and headed for Hong Kong for three days of liberty. When we were in port, the admiral let the flag Marines know if one of us would accompany him. If he was not going to meet with someone concerning the Navy or a dignitary, he put on his civvies and told us to stand down.

The admiral was a good man. Once, when the ship's water system was down we had to take four-minute showers. A master at arms stood by each shower with a stopwatch. The admiral stood in line just like one of the crew, waiting his turn. He had a shower stall in his cabin but there he stood, taking his turn with the rest of us.

Late in the afternoon during the first week of August, the *News* dropped anchor in the bay between Hong Kong and Kowloon. That night, as I stood on the port side the lights of the city reflected off the water. It was incredibly beautiful as Chinese junks and sampans made their way across the well-lit swells toward Kowloon.

Danny and I boarded a water taxi that took us to the dock where we hailed down a trishaw.

"Take us to the Peninsula Hotel."

While we waited for our meal, I made my way to the head. The restroom was ornate with colorful tile everywhere. The urinals went all the way to the floor and were also covered in tile. Standing, I thought I heard a noise. I looked around and saw no one. A moment went by, and I heard it again. Looking to my right and down, I saw an old Chinese woman. She was squatted down and backed into the urinal. She smiled, then I smiled. I finished up, washed my hands, and walked out. At the door, I turned back for one more look. She was still there, smiling.

"Danny, you're not going to believe what just happened!"

I told him about it as we walked to the bar. On the far wall was a huge aquarium. It had to be twelve feet tall and twenty feet long. You could see it from any table in the room. It was colorful, soothing, and mesmerizing.

The room was crowded with local Brits and their girlfriends, Aussies, a few sailors, and other Marines from the *News*.

I sat there nursing a whiskey when a beautiful Chinese girl walked by my table. She had long dark hair past her shoulders. She wore a black miniskirt with a white blouse. I immediately put out my hand. Danny had wandered off, so I was alone.

"Would you like to sit down and have a drink with me?"

"Yes, thank you."

Her English was very good. Her name was Lynn. She worked for the British government. Her mother was French. She had two brothers. One brother was a cop in Hong Kong. The other one was in school in Japan.

Then, it was my turn. She wanted to know about Oklahoma. Why did I join the Corps? Did I think the war would last much longer?

We saw each other one more time before the *News* sailed. She admittedly was on my mind for some time. Soon, I hoped to get back to Hong Kong. It never happened. We never saw each other again.

My time aboard the *News* was pretty much routine. We took rounds from shore batteries during fire missions, but we were never hit. The NVA pretty much stopped the WBLCs from Hainan Island. The night fighters took their toll.

Yokosuka -Sasebo-Tokoyo Hotsie Baths

Being aboard the *News*, I got back to Yokosuka, Japan one more time. For two American dollars, the Japanese had wonderful baths called Hotsie Baths. You went in and paid your two dollars, then two scantily clad Japanese girls helped you undress. They put you in a large bathtub of very hot water. They used a soft cloth and brush to completely wash you, adding hot water from a bucket as needed to keep the water hot. At first, you had to ease into the tub because it was so hot. After rinsing off with more hot water, you stepped out. They directed you to sit on a small stool.

After Danny and I sat there fresh out of the tub, the girls came up behind us and poured a bucket of cold water on our heads and shoulders. They then ran away laughing and giggling. When that cold water hit us after sitting in that hot bath for twenty to thirty minutes, we both stood up yelling and cursing. I have to admit though, it was quite invigorating.

Right after we got our clothes on and stepped outside in the cold, damp, foggy air, we looked at each other and said, "Let's do it again."

So, we went back inside, knowing full-well what was coming. The Japanese knew how to take a bath.

* * *

In late November 1967, the *News* docked at Subic Bay. We boarded a C-141 Starlifter at Clark Air Force base and headed back to the states. Our six-month tour was over. When everyone on the plane settled down, I thought about the places I'd been and probably would never see again: Alaska, Singapore, Hong Kong, Yokosuka, Sasebo, Tokyo, Manilla, and the Coast of Vietnam.

Little did I know that in six months, I would be back.

The big C-141 landed at the Marine base at El Toro about two in the morning. We put our gear on the bus. I slept most of the way to Long Beach. That bunk was going to feel awfully good. I hoped I didn't have duty the next day.

It took several days to adjust to the time difference, but before long everything was back to normal.

We had been back in town a couple of days when Danny and I decided to go into Long Beach. The plan was to get a drink and maybe pick up a couple of girls. We walked through the door and two nice-looking girls sat at the bar. We looked at each other—*timing is everything*.

Introducing ourselves, we proceeded to lay as much bullshit on 'em as was needed. Both were cute, wore short skirts, and seemed to be generally interested. But the girl next to me hardly smiled. Danny and I kept them laughing but, again I noticed the girl next to me hardly opened her mouth, not saying much at all. Danny suddenly said something that made the girl next to me laugh. That's when I saw it. When her upper lip raised above her teeth, there it was. She had a hole in one of her front teeth. It looked like somebody had shot a BB through it. There was black around the edges of the hole. That immediately cooled my heels. I tried not to stare but it was hard not to. My first thought was that we needed to go.

"Well, Danny. We need to be getting back to the base."

"What are you talking about? We don't need to get back."

I stood up, grabbed him by the arm and squeezed it tight. "Danny, we need to go! Now, right now!"

He saw it in my eyes, something was wrong. We told the girls goodnight and headed out the door.

Once outside he said, "What the fuck is the matter with you? Everything was going great. This better be good."

"Danny, the girl had a hole in her tooth. I kept wondering why she hardly smiled, then you said something that cracked her up. She laughed hard, and I saw it. She's got a hole through one of her front teeth. Man, it was clear through and black on the edges. There was no way I was going to hook up with her. Now do you understand?"

"Yeah, I get it. I'm not happy about it, but I get it."

"What if she had been sitting on the stool next to you, she smiled, and you saw it?"

"You got a point. But hell, I would have reached over to the other girl and said why don't you sit over here?"

"I get it, now. You would have traded—putting the girl with the bad teeth on me."

"Something like that."

"You motherfucker! Come on. Let's look for a ride back to the base."

The night was cool as we stepped into the street looking for a ride.

* * *

It was the middle of December 1967. I was taking the admiral's car to Los Angeles. I pulled away from the dock next to the *Bryce Canyon*. I made my way down the two-lane road for about a half-a-mile. It was the only connection between the ships at anchor and the Long Beach Naval Station.

As Time Goes By: One Marine's Story

Off to the right, I noticed a sailor walking alone on the small shoulder. Slowing down I leaned over and rolled down the window.

"Hey, you need a ride?"

"Yeah, sure. Thanks, man."

He told me his name was Reggie, and he was going to the PX.

"I'm going right by there," I said.

His ship, a destroyer, docked the day before. In a few days he would be going back home to St Louis for Christmas.

"Where you from?" he asked.

"Oklahoma. Tulsa, Oklahoma. I've got another week before I fly out."

"Where did you get this car?"

I'm a flag Marine for a rear admiral. He and his wife are going to a dinner in LA tomorrow night. I have to check the route and driving time so everything goes smoothly."

As I pulled up in front of the PX, Reggie leaned over, shook my hand, and got out.

"Thanks, man. I really appreciate this."

"You bet, Reggie. Enjoy your leave and have a good Christmas."

About four weeks later after the new year, I was walking down the street in Long Beach. Looking up, I saw Reggie coming toward me. He noticed me about the same time. With a huge grin on his face, we shook hands.

"How was Christmas? How's your family doing? Everything good?"

"Yeah, man. Everything was great. Are you hungry?"

"I could eat."

"Come on. I know this great place. You like catfish?"

"You know I do."

As the two of us walked down a side street, I heard what sounded like a woman screaming. I looked at Reggie.

"Did you hear that?"

"Yeah, I did. I think it came from that alley just up there."

When we got to the alley, two black men were punching a young boy while the girl, standing a few feet away was jumping up and down, screaming.

As I started up the alley, Reggie grabbed my left arm and pulled me back. For the time it takes for one heartbeat, I thought Reggie had turned on me. In the time it took for that second heartbeat, Reggie looked at me.

"I'll handle this!"

He moved up the alley toward the two black men. He grabbed the first one, putting his left hand to the back of the man's neck and in the same move grabbed the man's right arm, lifted him up and threw him into the wall on the opposite side.

The alley was very narrow. A car could have driven through it but there was little room to open the car door. Reggie was a big man, over six feet and easily weighed over 200 pounds.

As soon as the black man got to his feet, he yelled at Reggie. "What are you doing man. I'm black. You're black. Why are you getting in the middle of this?"

"The only similarity between you and me is the pigment of our skin. Now get outta here!"

I was a little disappointed in myself for just a moment. Yes, Reggie was black. When he grabbed my arm, I thought the worst. I was wrong. When the girl calmed down, they both thanked Reggie. The young boy shook my hand. Before long I lost sight of them as they walked in the direction of the Pike—an amusement park down on the beach.

"I hope you're still hungry."

"Like I said before, I could eat!"

One regret I have thought about many times was Reggie. I wish we had kept in touch. He was a rare man. I trusted him and that does not come easy for me.

A couple of weeks later, I was in downtown Long Beach just a few blocks from the main drag where I hoped to thumb a ride back to the base. The chow was always good aboard the *Bryce Canyon* but every so often I liked to go into town and eat at Milos—a family restaurant that had great catfish. With the street all but deserted, I started to cross the intersection against the light.

Just as I stepped off the curb, two men on the opposite corner hollered, "Hey, don't cross that street. The light hasn't changed yet."

I hollered back, "I'll cross the fucking street whenever I want."

Hearing what I said both men began jogging, closing the distance between us.

I quickly made it across the street, threw off my jacket, and backed up to a brick wall. I didn't want either of them to get behind me.

One of the men was tall and lanky. The other looked like he hadn't missed too many meals. As they closed in, the tall one put on a pair of black gloves. If I took him out first while keeping my eye on the other one, maybe, just maybe the other one wouldn't have the stomach for a fight.

As the tall one closed in, he obviously had the better reach on me with his long arms. He seemed overconfident and swung wild like a windmill. I took a chance. I moved in quick and kicked him on the inside of his right knee at the joint. He buckled and wretched in pain. Throwing a quick left hook to his mouth, he went down.

As I lunged toward the second man, I lost my balance grabbing him. We both fell onto the asphalt. Just as we were rolling on the street, a city bus pulled up to us with the driver laying on his horn. The bus was just a few feet away. As I stood up, I saw the fat boy trying to catch up with his friend—who was already across the street, limping as he ran. I noticed a metal basket on the edge of the curb. It was the kind of basket paper boys kept their newspapers in. I went to grab it with the intention of throwing it at them as I chased them down the sidewalk.

When I flung it at the two men, I didn't realize it had a couple of bricks inside. As the bricks came flying out, I felt a surge of pain from my right shoulder. After rubbing my arm, I picked up one of the bricks and hurled it through the air. I caught the fat boy in the back. The sound of the brick hitting him made a sound like the 'whump' you hear when you beat a rug hanging on the line outside to loosen the dust. He stopped and turned looking at me as I ran toward him. He turned again and both men ran away, down the sidewalk.

As I stood there, catching my breath, a young boy and his friend came running up to me.

"You are a Marine, aren't you?"

"Yes, I am."

He turned to his friend, "See? I told you. Give me a quarter!"

I kind of grinned as I walked down the sidewalk to the main drag. Hopefully, I could thumb a ride back to base.

When I woke the next morning, I decided to go back into Long Beach to have a good breakfast and see a movie since I didn't have duty until late in the evening. After a shower and a shave, I remembered a small coffee shop not far from where I had run into trouble the night before.

I walked into the coffee shop. There were no tables, just stools at the bar. I smelled the coffee as I walked through the door. As I sat there, fumbling with my napkin, I bumped my right thumb against the counter.

In a low voice, "Damn." Somehow, I had jammed my right thumb the previous night. It throbbed.

A girl sitting next to me politely asked, "Are you all right?"

"Last night I got into it with two guys just across the street."

"Was that you about six o'clock, just across the street?"

"Yes."

"We both work at the bank nights. We were just getting back to work when we saw it all." Her friend was sitting next to her.

"My name's Bruce. I had just had dinner when those two jumped me."

"My name is Marilyn. Marilyn Wayne."

The three of us sat there and talked as we ate our breakfast. Needless to say, I couldn't believe my luck. I asked her out. She accepted.

Marilyn and I dated for the next five months. She was easy on the eyes, petite, with short blond hair. She had her own car. We went out together every chance we could, usually to dinner or a movie. One night we went to LA to see the Lennon Sisters who sung on *The Lawrence Welk Show*. Another night we sat in the audience of *The Newlywed Game* at the studio.

Christmas was coming up. I got basket leave to go home. She wasn't happy about it, but she understood. At the airport, we said our good-byes, and I promised to call her the following day.

The plane arrived in Tulsa. The old man was there to pick me up. We both acted like we were glad to see each other. It felt good to be home. While in Hong Kong, I'd bought him a nice camera. I bought my stepmother china, and Mr. Gardner a set of pearls for his wife.

Before I left to go overseas, I got a short leave. Mr. Gardner and I were sitting in his kitchen having coffee. His daughter, Kathy and

I weren't dating any longer. He and I had become good friends. I still owed him a little money he had loaned me at Christmas, so I asked if there was anything he wanted me to pick up for him while I was overseas.

"Some nice pearls. Some nice, cultured pearls."

When we were in Hong Kong, I went to the Fleet Locker Club in search of pearls. The chief told me that was the place to buy pearls in Hong Kong.

"You won't get taken at the Fleet Locker Club."

I drove to Mr. Gardner's house on Christmas Eve just before dark. I knocked on the door. Kathy answered.

"Hello, come in."

"I need to speak to your dad."

"He's in the kitchen."

I walked into the kitchen. There sat Mr. Gardner, having coffee.

"Hello. Come in, come in. Want a cup of coffee?"

"No, thank you, sir. I've got something for you."

I showed him the red velvet box. He opened it. His face became a little flushed. I knew he would be pleased. The box held a necklace and two earrings of Mickey Motto pearls, the best cultured pearls in the world.

"They're beautiful, just beautiful. Where did you get them?"

"Hong Kong."

"These are obviously worth more than what you owed me. Let me pay you for them."

"No, Mr. Gardner. I could never pay what I owe you."

We shook hands and he walked me to the door. Once outside, I remember thinking to myself that for once in my life I didn't say too much or too little. For once, I said just what needed to be said.

It was Christmas Eve. Marilyn was probably wondering why I hadn't yet called her. On the way home I thought about her. I hoped her Christmas had been as good as mine.

My leave was over. The old man drove me to the airport. We said our good-byes and shook hands. I boarded the aircraft. As the plane gained altitude, I had no idea that in about four months I would be back in Tulsa. My job in the Corps was about to take a drastic change.

Marilyn met me at the airport in LA. As we drove back to Long Beach, she asked a lot of questions. Did I have a good time? Did I see some of my old friends? Was Mr. Gardner surprised? Had my stepdad and I gotten along? and so on. I told her it went fine but I was glad to be back. It was where I belonged. She seemed to like that.

Home for Christmas

4

STAGING BATTALION

"Every man's life ends the same way. It is only the details of how he lived and how he died that distinguish one man from another." ~ Ernest Hemingway.

I GOT BACK TO LONG BEACH a couple of days after the New Year. Taking up my regular duties with the admiral, I sat on the bunk in our little cubbyhole. Danny walked in and sat on a chair next to me.

"What are you reading?"

"It's an article about the war."

When I looked up, I couldn't help but notice Danny had several new ribbons on his chest.

"Danny, why are you wearing a Bronze Star and a Presidential Citation on your blouse? We haven't seen any combat."

"My parents expect me to come home a hero, so I wore these ribbons home."

"You would think they would be glad just to get you home in one piece. You shouldn't be wearing those, Danny."

"At least *I* know who my father is."

Anger built up inside me. He threw in my face something I had told him when we were probably drunk in Singapore or Hong Kong. I grabbed him by his blouse and jerked him out of his chair. I lost control.

Dragging him outside the room and into the passageway, I threw him to the deck.

Someone hollered, "Attention on deck."

I released Danny and came to attention. Almost immediately the chief of staff was standing in front of me.

"You're an embarrassment to the admiral. You're out of here." He told the other Marine to drive me over to the barracks, get my gear, and to report to the Marine barracks.

"Aye-aye, sir."

As I settled into the barracks life, I got to know the other Marines and learned my new duties.

It came together. That was where I belonged. There were no regrets. If I hadn't gotten kicked off the admiral's staff at some point, I would've asked for a change of duty.

The experiences I had working for the admiral were invaluable. I learned a lot about myself. I had seen places I might have never otherwise seen.

If the chief of staff hadn't stepped in, I could have easily wound up in the brig. When I grabbed Danny, with the rage I was feeling I wanted to hurt him. At that moment, he had conjured up the pain and hurt that had been building up inside of me for years.

About a week later as I walked down a sidewalk in downtown Long Beach, Danny walked up to me. I was not in a forgiving mood.

In three to four weeks my orders would be coming through, back to the FMF (Fleet Marine Force), Vietnam.

"Hey, look. All you need to do is go to the chief of staff, tell him what happened. I'm sure he'll give you your job back."

"Can't do it, Danny. Besides why don't you tell him what happened? I'm going where I belong. At first, I thought being a flag Marine was good duty. A lot of Marines would like to have it, but I don't belong there. I'm sure there are going to be times when I'll wish I was back with the admiral but I signed up for the Marines. That's where I'm going."

"Come on, let's get something to drink."

"You go ahead. I've got other plans. Some other time."

As we separated, I saw Danny just one more time before my orders came through. I was on the main gate at the Naval base, checking cars in and out.

As the admiral's car approached me, I stood at attention and saluted. Danny was driving.

As he passed by, he made sure I noticed that on his left arm was another stripe. He had made corporal. I'm sure his parents were very proud.

When my orders came through, I took a bus to Camp Pendleton.

Marilyn wanted to drive me there, but I thought it would be easier on both of us if we said our good-byes in Long Beach. I assured her I would call the first chance I got, and I would write to her often.

Staging lasted about four weeks. I made squad leader. The sergeant in charge of my platoon was a battalion recon Marine.

On the weekends if we got liberty, I got on a bus for Long Beach. Marilyn would drive me back. During the third week, one of the Marines in my squad was giving me trouble. I went to my sergeant to ask if he had any suggestions about how to best handle it.

When I told him what was going on, all he said was, "Deck him."

"Deck him?"

"Deck him."

Lance Corporal Redus with his squad.

I liked that sergeant. He was a no-nonsense type. I would handle it.

The next day, the whole platoon was sitting outside of a mock Vietnamese village waiting for our turn to go in and run infantry tactics. We were there to watch the platoon in front of us to learn from their mistakes. The Marine I'd had a problem with was sitting about two bodies from me. He was making jokes and laughing out loud.

I told him, "Hey, hold it down."

"Fuck you."

I got up and walked back to where he was sitting. "Stand up."

When he stood up, I hit him in the jaw. Down he went.

"Don't get back up. Stay down."

He stayed on the ground. Two officers, a colonel and a Marine captain suddenly came running up.

"What's going on here?"

Just as suddenly as the two officers came up, my platoon sergeant showed up. I remember thinking to myself, *You're in real trouble now. You've done it again.* No sooner did that thought enter my mind, the sergeant spoke up.

"I've got this under control, sir."

The colonel, with a stern look on his face, looked at me then faced my sergeant.

"Fine, sergeant."

The two officers walked away. The sergeant looked at me with a slight smile. I decided right then and there I would follow that sergeant anywhere. He had taken up for me. That had never happened before.

With staging behind us, we got two weeks leave. The day before going home, a Marine captain had us assemble on the bleachers just outside our barracks. With a light drizzle falling, he walked the length of the bleachers, then stood there, staring at us.

"Tomorrow, you men will be going on leave. You each have two weeks. In those two weeks, see your families, talk to your friends, do everything you want to do because some of you are not coming back."

I remember all eyes were on him. It was so quiet you could hear light rain hit the bill of our covers. Everyone, including me, was thinking the same thing.

"I'm gonna make it. I know I will."

The Marine on my left was thinking that, too, but he would be dead in two months. A box mine was going to kill him and another

Marine on Hill 88. He would not suffer. There would be no pain. It would break every bone in his body.

Standing by the guard shack at Pendleton, I waited for Marilyn. She insisted on taking me to the LA airport. When she drove up, a lot of heads turned. A few whistled. I looked back and smiled. How lucky I was to have someone like her to come for me.

"Now, you promise to call me."

"Sure Mar, I'll call as soon as I get home. I'll call at least a few times before I come back."

"Now, you know you promised to come back a few days before you have to report back in so we can spend time together."

"I promise I'll call you as soon as I know what day I know my flight is scheduled. Then, you pick me up and we'll spend time together. I promise."

At the airport, I checked in my duffel bag and got my ticket. She and I hugged and kissed. They called for my flight to board. I had to go. I was going to miss her.

As I walked through the plane looking for my seat, checking it twice just to be sure, there was a pretty blond sitting in the window seat.

"Ma'am, I've checked this ticket twice. I think this is my seat."

"Please, sit down. You're a Marine aren't you?"

"Yes, ma'am."

We both sat there not saying much until the plane leveled off in flight.

She turned to me, "What's your name?"

"It's Bruce, ma'am but people call me JB."

"My name is Molly Bee."

"Molly Bee, I remember seeing you on *The Jimmy Dean Show*. You sing country music. I want to apologize for not recognizing you right off. My mind was somewhere else. The last thing I expected was to be sitting next to someone famous."

She was easy to talk to. The stewardess brought us snacks and a drink. I answered her questions about the Corps, and she told me about her career. The plane hit an air pocket and took a sudden drop. She grabbed my forearm.

"Ma'am, you've got strong fingers."

"It comes from playing the guitar for so long."

The hours between LA and Oklahoma City seemed to fly by. When the plane landed, she asked if I would walk her to her cab. The stewardess told me there was a layover of about thirty minutes. I had plenty of time. Outside the airport, we had no trouble hailing a cab. She turned to me as I put her bag in the backseat.

"Thank you so much for walking me to my cab." She was shorter than me, so she stood on her tiptoes and kissed me on the cheek. "Good luck, Marine."

"Thanks, Molly."

After a few moments, she was gone.

I enjoyed telling the story to other Marines. It always came up, "What was she wearing?"

"I've seen her on TV, too. She is a good-looking woman."

Sometimes I would tell the boys she hugged me then kissed me on the cheek. It never happened that way, but I don't think she would mind.

The ol' man picked me up at the airport in Tulsa. Two weeks seemed like forever, but it went by faster than I thought it would. David, my old boss let me work for him while I was home. I needed the money to pay for my ticket back to California.

I went out with a few old friends, jogged every day to stay in shape, called Marilyn and then just laid around the house thinking. Thinking probably wasn't a good idea but I couldn't help it. The clouds, the sky, the birds, and the trees seemed more beautiful than before. I had taken so much for granted in my life. In a short time, I would be facing men who wanted to take it from me. It was hard to explain. I wanted to go back early, spend time with Marilyn but something kept nagging at me. I wanted to stay positive. I would make it back to look at the sky, the clouds, the trees, and the birds, my friends, my family but the thought that would not go away about death was a black cloud hanging over me.

I had to get up early because my flight left at seven o'clock. Just as I was ready to walk out the front door, my little sister came running out of her room and threw her arms around my waist.

"Don't go, please don't go. I had a bad dream. I dreamed you got killed!" She had tears in her eyes.

I had to make her understand. I held her close.

"Look, I'm gonna be all right. Before you know it, I'll be back. I'll write to you. Now dry your eyes and get back in bed. I love you."

The ol' man and my stepmother drove me to the airport. We shook hands. I hugged her and got on the plane.

Luckily, I got a window seat. The plane picked up speed and banked to the left. The sun was up. The Arkansas River shone like a sheet of glass. In a little over a year, I would be back. I knew I'd make it.

Taking a direct flight from Tulsa to LA, we landed in the mid-afternoon. I called Marilyn the night before, giving her my flight details. She sounded excited.

Over the phone was not the time to break her heart. I had to do that face-to-face. Even then she wouldn't understand.

How do I explain to her I had a bad feeling I am not going to make it back? Tulsa was my home. I needed to stay as long as I could. *How do I explain that to her?* I wasn't sure I understood it myself.

When I got off the plane, there she was, waiting in the lobby. We hugged and kissed. I got my gear from the conveyor belt and walked to her car. It was then I told her I didn't have any days left. I had to report to Camp Pendleton that day.

She cried. She didn't understand. She asked if there was someone else. I told her no, there wasn't anyone else.

We got on the highway and headed down the coast toward Oceanside.

It wasn't long before I spotted a greyhound bus. Speeding up, we got ahead of it and pulled to the side of the road. Jumping from the car, I signaled the bus driver to pull over. He flashed his lights.

As I grabbed my gear, Marilyn was still in tears. It broke my heart to leave her.

The driver appeared at the back of the bus.

"We've got to go, son."

"Give me a minute. I'll be right there."

Marilyn and I hugged and kissed.

"I'll write the first chance I get." I turned toward the bus, looked back once.

That was the last time I ever saw her.

* * *

Lying on my bunk, I couldn't sleep. I just lay there thinking about the next day.

We flew out of El Toro. It was better than spending two weeks on a troop ship with guys puking. We first flew to Hawaii, then Okinawa, and finally Phu Bai, Vietnam.

Dan and JB off the coast of the Philippines

5

AMBUSH

*"There are no great men, only great challenges that
ordinary men are forced by circumstances to meet."
~ Fleet Admiral William F. "Bull" Halsey Jr.*

A FTER WE LANDED IN OKINAWA, they bused us to several
rows of barracks. We were told going outside for a smoke
was allowed but not to wander off. The chow hall was at
the end of the barracks. And, by the way, "You're probably going
to be here for two to three days before your flight takes off."

Having several hundred of us crammed into the barracks for
days, tempers flared, fights broke out—the waiting was the hardest
part. On the third day, we loaded up the buses and headed for the
flight line. It would be the last leg of our journey.

The plane was quiet. There was very little talking, no joking
around. Most were in solemn thought. Every man looked out his
own window.

I was in an aisle seat. About an hour into our flight, my platoon
sergeant from staging suddenly knelt down beside me.

"If I can get you into my unit, will you come?"

"You bet. You bet I would!"

"There's no guarantee, but I'll try. I'll catch up with you in Phu Bai and let you know one way or the other."

"Right, Sarg. And thanks!"

He patted me on the shoulder as he stood up and walked back to his seat. *Imagine that!* He was gonna try to get me into his battalion recon unit. It sounded exciting. I hoped he would be successful.

As we neared Vietnam, rumors made their way through the aircraft. One of the Marines told me, "The gooks are mortaring the airfield at Phu Bai. The plane's gonna slow down just enough for us to get off. Then, it's going to take off again."

I looked at him and told him I doubted it was true. I reassured him we would probably be all right.

Sure enough, the landing went smooth—no mortars, just Marines who had done their tour waiting to get on board the plane for the trip back to the States.

As we each stepped down the ramp at the rear of the plane, the four stewardesses stood there, kissing each of us on the cheek as we walked by.

I stepped off the ramp. The heat and humidity hit me. For a brief moment, I closed my eyes. I could have sworn I was back in Houston.

We were herded into an airplane hanger, where light paperwork waited for us. I kept looking up, hoping to see the sergeant. He struck me as a man of his word. There wasn't a man in the Corps I'd rather share a piece of ground with. Just as I signed my name for the last time, I looked up. He came toward me. He wasn't wearing his good-news face.

"Redus, I'm sorry. I talked to my CO He said they really need grunts, now. He wouldn't let me bring anyone into the unit."

"That's all right, Sarg. I understand. It just wasn't meant to be. Thanks for trying."

As he turned to walk away, he turned around and stuck out his hand. "Keep your head down, Marine."

"You bet, Sarg, you bet."

As he walked out of the hanger I remember thinking, *I hope we both come out of this in one piece.*

Another NCO hollered, "All you men. As I read off your name and company, form up over here."

I finally heard my name. "Redus, Golf Company—over there."

After the names had been read, another NCO motioned to us, "You men, follow me."

We grabbed our duffel bags and headed out. Before long, the sergeant pointed out a row of tents with wooden floors.

"This is our area. That hooch over there is the duty hut. Pick out a cot. This is gonna be your home—for a while, anyway. We're gonna keep you in the rear for a few days, issue your weapons, and take a couple of classes on booby traps. But the main reason in keeping you here is to let you get used to the heat and humidity. Tomorrow we're gonna go to the range and have you fan-fire your weapons. Now, drop off your gear. It's time for chow. The corporal will show you the way. Don't worry, no one is gonna bother your gear."

After chow, I wandered around. I remembered feeling a little self-conscious. Most of the Marines we ran into, their utilities were a faded green. Their jungle boots were roughed up. Ours were new. We stuck out like new pennies.

* * *

It was our last night in the rear. The next morning right after chow, we were to report to the duty hut in full gear. I was restless, couldn't sleep. I took a walk with my weapon in hand. Moving from one line of tents to another, I suddenly found myself standing in front of a Quonset hut. Over the door, it read CHAPEL.

During the two days I had been in Vietnam, it never once crossed my mind to seek out the chapel. Religion never played a big part in my life. When I opened the door, a blast of cool air hit me in the face. Air conditioning—the chapel had air conditioning. Inside, I shut the door behind me.

No one was there. I was alone.

Placing my weapon against the wall, I took off my cover and placed it over the barrel. I walked past row after row of chairs. There was a table on a small stage with a large bible and a metal cross. There had been no planning on my part to seek out God, and yet there I was.

It's probably a good time to make amends.

People seem to turn to religion when they're in trouble. Approaching the stage, I got past the first step and went to my knees not sure about what to say. I knew God loved all men, but my job was to kill men. That was the dilemma. I settled with asking God to please forgive me for my sins. I thanked him for the people who had been important in my life, and I left.

I don't know how much good I did. But as I headed back to my company area it felt like the slate was clean. The next day I was going into the bush. If God wanted me, he would know where to find me. *We shall see what is written.*

It was 0700 and the new replacements stood in front of the duty hut. Gunny told us to take off our pack and stand behind it. He worked his way down the line, going through each pack—taking out whatever he felt we didn't need.

"If any of you men have shaving lotion or toothpaste in your packs, take it out and throw it on the ground. When you shave, just use water. You men will brush your teeth using just water. The gooks don't care if your breath is fresh. Remember that pack is gonna be on *your* back. It's going to dig into your shoulders. You're gonna be carrying extra canteens, ammunition, grenades, food, an extra mortar round or two, a flak jacket, a poncho, your steel pot and writing material, envelopes, and your weapon. I don't want any man to drop out because he's carrying gear he doesn't need. Now get in the truck."

No sooner had we sat down in the back in two rows of metal seats, a Marine stood up and stuck his head through a hole in the roof where a .30 caliber machine gun set on a swivel.

"If we get hit on the left, get out on the right and return fire. If we get hit on the right, get out on the left and return fire. Got it?"

We let out a low, "Yeah, we got it."

We went through several checkpoints. We finally hit an asphalt road, Route 1.

We drove fast and made it to Freedom Bridge. Ten minutes later the deuce-and-a-half made its way up Hill 88. We were home.

Jumping off the truck, a sergeant came up.

"You men form up over here. The captain wants to have a word with you."

We moved to where the captain stood.

"You men can take a knee if you want. The smoking lamp is lit. First, you're here. Accept it. There's no such thing as a million-dollar wound. There's only two ways for you to leave here—walk out or get carried out.

"If you are talking to an officer, do not, I repeat do not stand at attention or salute. Take off your skivvies. We don't wear them. Use them to clean your weapon. Take the sling off your weapon. That weapon should always be in your hands. Do not lay it down and walk off. If I find a weapon lying around, I can promise you, you won't do it again.

"Put no more than eighteen rounds in a magazine, not twenty. We've found we have less trouble with a weapon feeding the chamber. Don't cinch up your helmet straps. Let them hang or cinch them up tight to the back of your helmet. Squad leaders will have black tape. Put it over the swivels where the sling attaches to your weapon—below the barrel and on the butt. Also, tape your dog tags together so there is no noise from them hitting each other.

"Twice a week your squad leader will pass around a bore rod to help keep your weapons clean. Remember your weapon is your life. Now, this is important men. Pay attention to your fire team leaders and squad leaders. They'll teach you things you didn't learn at staging. That's all I have. Gunny will fill you men in on which squad to report to."

"Redus, you're in Riley's squad."

"Which one is Riley?"

"He's the splib standing over there."

After I met Riley and the other Marines in the squad, my dog tags and the swivels on my weapon needed to be taped down.

My fire team leader, Dennis Studenny told me to get some sleep after I got my gear squared away.

* * *

That night we moved out after dark to set up an ambush. And so, it began. On an ambush when I wasn't on watch, it was a chance to grab a little sleep.

The next night, my fire team was outside the wire again. We set up in a tree line next to a creek. The gooks had already set in on the opposite creek bank before we got there. Rounds landed around us. Cussing and moving at the same time, we quickly found a ditch and returned fire.

We took no hits but somebody suddenly hollered, "Mortars."

Then, a loud boom was followed by another. The mortar crew didn't have us bracketed yet.

Dennis gave us a loud whisper, "Let's get the fuck out of here."

The four of us headed deeper into the jungle, trying not to lose anyone. We stopped every few minutes and counted heads. Dennis got on the radio and told the Marines inside the wire we were coming in.

They told us when we were about a hundred yards out to pop a green flare. They would hold their fire.

Taking cover in a ditch, I stepped out holding the flare in my left hand, hitting it on the bottom with my helmet. The sky suddenly lit up green. As the sky lit up, Dennis reached out and knocked my feet out from under me. I had no sooner hit the ground when he grabbed me and dragged me into the ditch. He got close to my face and with a loud whisper again—

"You dumb son-of-a-bitch. You can't stand out there in that light. If the gooks are out there, you're making a target of yourself. They'll know where we are."

"You're right, Dennis."

All Marines are a little bit crazy. Lesson learned. It was my second night.

The radio crackled, "Come on in."

We ran for the wire.

One of the Marines jumped up from his machine gun and pulled back the razor wire and quietly said, "We heard shooting. Did you see anything out there?"

"Yeah, they must have seen us when we were setting in. They had a mortar crew. We were lucky."

* * *

That was the second time in my life somebody shot at me. Before, it was an irate farmer. This was different.

As the days turned to weeks, I learned a lot from Dennis. At first, I tried to stay clean, then I gave up. I accepted the dirt and sweat just like I accepted sleeping on the ground every night. It was the monsoon season. It constantly rained day and night. Out on patrol or on ambush at night— we were amazed at what we got used to. Inside the wire, we put on ponchos. Outside the wire on ambush or on killer teams, we learned to live with it—no poncho. We were gonna get wet. When our watches were over, we lay down in the grass or mud, closed our eyes, and went to sleep.

Combat in Vietnam was hard, both mentally and physically. It tested your faith. It was bloody. It smelled. And, it was dirty. Nothing got us ready for combat. It was baptism by fire. There were no dress rehearsals, no second chances or do overs. If you think you might have some idea what it was like, forget it. You're not even close.

Sherman or 'Uncle Billy'—a name given to him by his men— said, "War is cruelty." He told his men, "Make them fear and dread us," as he burned Atlanta and began his march to the sea to Savannah.

To the Roman Legions, "Their exercises were bloodless wars, and their wars were bloody exercises."

Nothing can prepare you for combat, not the months you spent in boot camp, or the months spent going through infantry tactics. When that first round comes stinging through the high grass or hitting the tree you're behind—the geysers that erupt around you as you run across a paddy looking for cover—the round you heard going by your head—the Marine lying face down with the side of his head gone, hollering as you run—

"You motherfuckers! You motherfuckers!"

Telling yourself not to stop. *Don't stop. This is a kill box. You've got to get to cover, firing your weapon as you run. You've got to find cover or you're going to die here.*

In Vietnam, death was a big part of your life. If you worried about it, if you thought about it too much, you could never handle the stress.

One of the Marines in another squad told me,

"If you can get through the first two months, you've got a good chance of getting through your tour alive."

I wanted to believe him, like some rule of thumb. But as time went on, I saw Marines with eight to ten months in country go down in that shit hole. All I could think about was I knew they were dead. In a few days, a Marine was going to be knocking on their family's door. The news would be devastating.

* * *

It was late in the afternoon. Dennis was talking to Gunny. We had been on patrol most of the day—hadn't seen a thing. Besides, it was our turn to be inside the wire that night. I would heat up chow, then find me a spot to get a full night's sleep. It was about that time Dennis came walking up to me.

"I just got the word. They are moving me to blooper man, and you're taking over the fire team."

"You gotta be shitting me."

"No. Gunny just told me, and now I'm telling you. And that's not all. You're gonna love this. The captain decided this new lieutenant we've got needs to go out on ambush to gain experience. Captain wants to send three fire teams, a machine gun team, a corpsman, a radioman, and me with the blooper."

"That's eighteen men! We never send out that many for one ambush."

"I know. But the captain wants to make sure we have plenty of firepower since the lieutenant will be with us. Go get your men ready. We're heading out in about ten minutes."

We checked our gear, filled our canteens, and moved toward the captain.

The lieutenant had been on the hill for about two days. I knew very little about him, but I respected his rank. Hopefully the night would be quiet. The lieutenant would get experience. We would be back on the hill the next morning. What could go wrong?

It would be dark in about three hours, so we had plenty of time to find a spot and sit in for the night. We were about twenty feet off a trail that led to a small village just over the horizon. My fire team was first, then a second fire team. The lieutenant, radio man, and corpsman were together. The machine gun crew was next and there was Dennis with his blooper on the end with the third fire team.

I had a good fire team. Dennis had seen to that.

I had just taken a bite of pound cake when the lieutenant stood up.

"If we see anything tonight, you don't fire until you hear the crack of my forty-five."

I got off the ground and walked over to the lieutenant. I knew he was new to our unit. I wanted to explain to him as respectfully possible how we set off an ambush.

"Lieutenant, in an ambush like this, usually the fire team leader on either end sets off the ambush. Once the gooks are in the Kill Zone. The fire team leader on that end will set it off."

"Marine, that is a direct order. No one fires until they hear the crack of my forty-five. Is that understood?"

"Aye-aye, sir."

I turned and walked back to my men, kind of shaking my head as I went—hopefully not enough for the lieutenant to see it. The Marines all heard him.

We hadn't had any contact for several days. There was no reason for me to think we would see anything that night. My fire team worked out the watch on our end. It was just starting to get dark. There would be no more talking until daylight.

We used hand signals. If we had to talk, it was always a whisper in the other man's ear.

We sat in grass and brush about two-and-a-half to three feet high. It was a clear night with lots of stars.

I looked up and I saw the Seven Sisters making their way across the sky. They were not new to me. They would be over Oklahoma in the fall.

I saw off in the distance a line of tracers that seemed to come out of nowhere. It was Puff the Magic Dragon—an old AC-47 with three 7.62 mini-guns, the same plane paratroopers jumped out of in WWII.

The moon was up. Except for large rocks off to the left my field of vision was excellent. In the jungle, it was hard to see more than a few feet at times. Hearing helped to detect movement. An animal moving through the jungle at night could be challenging to your nerves.

My watch was over. I made a quick 360 check around our ambush site as I shook Stevie. He sat up, rubbed his eyes, and looked at me.

Leaning over to him, I whispered in his ear, "Have you got it? Are you awake?"

He looked at me, nodded his head, and waved his hand. When I laid down, I watched him for a few minutes. Stevie was a good man, nothing to worry about. Closing my eyes, I fell asleep.

It didn't feel like I had been asleep long. Someone was shaking my shoulder. It was not my watch. Something was wrong.

As I sat up, Stevie leaned over to me and whispered in my ear.

He said just one word, "Listen."

As I sat there, I heard nothing. Looking at Stevie, I shrugged my shoulders.

He quickly put his hand up to his earlobe and pulled on it while at the same time pointing down the trail to the left.

I looked down the trail and listened.

There was nothing, and then suddenly there was a voice—a gook's voice.

I immediately checked my weapon, making sure the safety was off. The ejection port was open. It was on full auto.

Stevie and I woke the other two Marines. As they sat up, I stared into their faces. When I was sure I had their attention, I put my hand up to my mouth telling them to be quiet. Then I patted the top of my head—"danger". Pulling on my left earlobe meant to listen. I then pointed down the trail off my left shoulder.

As I looked down the line, there was movement. The other Marines had heard the voices, too. My first thought was it was probably villagers getting home late. If they had no weapons, we would not harm them. It couldn't be NVA or VC. They were more disciplined than that. The people coming toward us were having conversations between themselves—not in a whisper but in a normal voice.

The moon was full.

Suddenly, there they were. The moonlight was incredible. It was NVA. I kept telling myself over and over, I see it, but it was so hard to believe.

Those NVA soldiers walked along like they were back home. Several walked side-by-side. One had his weapon by the barrel on his shoulder.

I counted them as they walked by. There were eight regulars and one officer. The officer was last in line. He had on a small cover and a pistol on his hip. Several Marines were gonna claim the kill on that officer. They'd want that pistol.

As the NVA passed by, I knew it would be over in a matter of seconds. My breathing was labored. The adrenaline flowed. When the shooting stopped, I would go out there and count the bodies. We didn't want anyone to get away or be loose out there in the night.

As I watched the NVA enter our kill zone, I waited for the crack of the lieutenant's .45, mentally saying to myself over and over, *Do it! Do it now, lieutenant. Do it now!*

Nothing!

There was no crack of the lieutenant's .45. The men in my fire team looked at me. I shook my head, shrugged my shoulders as the voices of the NVA gradually disappeared in the dark. Signaling to the Marines I was going back to sleep, I lay down and closed my eyes. The lieutenant evidently knew something we didn't. I was sure he'd straighten it out in the morning.

At the time, I had no idea what the lieutenant had done was going to cost him his life.

Lying on the ground asleep, I suddenly heard voices. Someone was hollering. No one had shaken me to let me know something was up. It was the lieutenant taking big steps through the brush throwing his arms up.

He kept repeating, "Why didn't you shoot? Why didn't you open fire?"

"But lieutenant, you gave us a direct order not to fire until we heard the track of your forty-five."

"You didn't fire, so we didn't fire. You gave us a direct order, lieutenant."

"Marine, get on the radio and get me the captain, now!"

I was still shaking out cobwebs when I heard the lieutenant, "Sir, this is Lieutenant Moss. Sir, about eight to ten NVA passed this way last night. I think they're in the village just over the rise."

"Sir, yes sir."

When he got off the radio, he turned to us, "The captain and the rest of the platoon are coming to us. It is gonna take about forty-five minutes to an hour for them to get here so each of you fire team leaders put one man out for security. The rest stand down."

I acknowledged the lieutenant's order.

"Stevie, you go out there about forty yards. I'll send someone to relieve you in about twenty-five to thirty minutes. Keep your eyes open."

With security out, I sat down with Dennis. "What the fuck happened?"

"Hell, I almost pulled my trigger. My finger was on it just waiting. Marty, you were there with the lieutenant. What happened?"

"We heard the gooks well before they got in the kill zone. I shook the lieutenant. Then I shook him again. He wouldn't wake up. I got nervous when they got close. I was afraid they were going to hear me. I think everyone but the lieutenant was awake. I just couldn't wake him. He's not used to sleeping in the bush."

It had been almost an hour when we spotted the captain. There were two dusters with him.

A duster was like a small tank. It had two 40mm cannons with no turret. The guns on the dusters reminded me of the small cannons on the *St Paul* and *New Port News,* like pompom guns that intermittently fired.

We stood around for a few minutes. I waved the security back in while the lieutenant and the captain walked a few yards away to have a talk. There wasn't any hollering but I felt the captain with his hands on his hips and the lieutenant's body language—there was an ass-chewing going on. They kept their voices low so we couldn't hear. It didn't take long. They broke it off and called the squad leaders over.

Soon Riley was back.

"Redus, the dusters are going to stay outside the village taking up station on the North and South side to catch anyone trying to escape. They'll each have a squad covering them. The rest of us are going into the village. You take your fire team into the village on the right. The rest of the squad will follow you. The other squad is going in on the left side with the captain and the lieutenant. Everybody got it? Any questions?"

"No."

I gathered my fire team.

"All right. We are going into the village on the right. Keep your distance, walk where I walk. Everybody got it? No questions? Check your weapons and keep your eyes open."

When we got to the edge of the village. I looked back.

"Keep your distance!"

Any time I went through a village I hadn't been in before or felt something wasn't right, I grabbed the first man or woman I came to.

There was a man standing off to the right, just outside the first hooch.

Grabbing him by his shirt, I told him, "Come on motherfucker, *La Di.*"

He didn't want to come, but he was coming with me none-the-less. I pulled him close—if there were any booby traps ahead, he would let me know if he hesitated to keep walking. Any gates we came to, he went up and opened first. Again, if he was hesitant I knew there was something there.

I looked back, "Keep your distance."

We were about halfway through the village when suddenly, BOOM! There was a big explosion off to my left. I immediately threw the villager to the ground as large clumps of dirt fell on me.

In the same instant, I looked back. My Marines were spread out in firing position. The next thing I heard was someone screaming. No shots were fired.

One of the Marines on my left hollered, "The lieutenant's hit. He stepped on a mine."

Quickly looking around, I pulled the villager to his feet.

Someone hollered, "Corpsman up."

Looking at the Marines around the lieutenant, I saw a bare bone sticking out. Yelling to my Marines, we continued to move through the village. There were no more explosions.

The captain gave the word, "Torch it."

A chopper came in outside the village for the lieutenant. No one else had taken a hit.

We blew up a small building made of concrete blocks and burned the village to the ground. The Vietnamese and what few animals they had were in a line heading down the trail away from the village. No shots were fired either by the Marines or the dusters but the villager's crops were destroyed as the dusters ran back and forth over them.

When we got back to the hill, I talked to the corpsman who worked on the lieutenant.

"How bad was it?"

"He lost both legs. The lieutenant kept saying, 'Help me get to my feet.' Hell man, his legs were gone. He lost a lot of blood and went into shock. He could have made it. He could have lived if he would have just remained calm. Before we landed at Da Nang he was gone. There was nothing more I could do."

About a week later, someone got a copy of *Stars and Stripes*. The lieutenant's name was in there. He was twenty-three years old and not married. It was his third day in the bush when he was killed.

On the hill there was relative safety. At times we had a tank or the dusters with us. If the platoon wasn't on an operation there were always patrols during the day and killer teams or ambush at night. You caught sleep whenever you could through rotation.

My fire team always looked forward to our turn inside the wire. When we were in the wire, we spread it out so everyone got good sleep. The platoon was shorthanded, but we made the best of it. There was little complaining. We were in it together.

When we went on patrol, I was constantly scanning the ground or paddy in front of me. The courage it took to walk the roads, hump the jungle, or wade through the rice paddies was incredible. Not knowing each step you took, or the Marine in front of you or behind you took could result in death or the loss of an arm or leg—or possible blindness.

Grace under Pressure. That was the way Hemingway described courage. At any point you could step on a mine, a punji pit, or step in a manhole filled with razor sharp pieces of bamboo, covered with human feces. You might hit a trip wire that released a grenade or caused the release of a dead fall from overhead that brought down a trap of punji stakes with the help of gravity. Anything could be booby-trapped. They were only limited by their imaginations.

Our squad was on patrol not far from the hill. I was on point with my Marines behind me, keeping their distance from each other. While scanning the ground in front of me, I stepped on the edge of a punji pit. As I felt my right foot caving in to the side of the hole, I quickly leaned to my left, catching my fall with my left hand.

Getting to my feet, I realized what a near miss that was. Lucky for me the gooks hadn't put another pit to the side. Sometimes they did that if a man were to step to the side to avoid stepping in a located pit.

Sensing there were more pits along the trail, I found a stick to probe my way. In total, there were eight more traps spaced about ten to twelve feet apart.

They dug the holes, lined the bottom with bamboo spears, and put strips of bamboo across the top about an inch below the ground. They then placed a piece of newspaper on the cross strips. They gently spread dirt and debris on the paper, making it impossible to see the pits.

Booby-traps were known as a weapon of the weak, not the strong. They were used to slow people down—to put fear in their enemy. It worked. We got fifty dollars a month extra for combat pay. It wasn't enough.

We left the hill after dark. The squad made its way to an ambush site. The shortest route took us through rice paddies. The moon was coming up. We were making a lot of noise. I was walking point and decided to head for the tree line. Riley sent a Marine up to tell me to get back online across the paddies.

I whispered in his ear, "You tell Riley I said to get fucked. The moon is up. Hell, it's like daylight out here. All the noise we're making splashing through this paddy—if there's a gook within eight hundred yards they know we're here. You go tell him that."

I turned and kept heading for the tree line. They followed. We set in for the night but saw nothing. When the fog burned off and the sun was over the trees, we headed back to the hill.

Walking point, I scanned ahead then quickly came back to the ground in front of me. Scanning both sides, just in front of me then back to the ground looking for anything out of place. As I looked to the left about forty feet ahead, something suddenly caught my attention.

Staring at it, I stopped.

Raising my left arm, everyone stopped.

Yelling at everyone to stay put, I moved in closer.

As I crept forward, there was a piece of green that didn't look natural. It stuck out like a barber's pole. Moving slowly, the trip wire became visible. Then I saw what had caught my eye. It was a law with two pounds of C-4 attached to it. I carefully moved a small limb and peered down the barrel of the law. It was full of American Grenades. My heart jumped into my throat as I hollered to Riley.

"Riley, get the fuck up here."

"What is it? What did you find?"

"Careful, the trip wire is right there. See it?"

"Fuckin' A. Yeah, man. I see it."

"Look at this. Two pounds of C-4 and that tube is full of American grenades. The com wire is attached to the grenade at the bottom. Look, I'm gonna go up the hill, get Gunny and tell him to call the engineers. You stay here, point out that trip wire to every man, and then leave someone here so some motherfucker doesn't come walking by and trip it."

How did they get in here so close to the hill? Hell, the wire's right there and the moon was out. What a crater that booby-trap would have made not to mention the explosion would probably have killed us. The gooks who set that booby-trap are probably watching us right now. Fuck 'em!

The next day my fire team patrolled an area east of the hill and worked our way to the creek that ran under Freedom Bridge. When we finally got to the bridge, I noticed an old man walking around with a wooden chair. He was holding onto it with one hand as it hung on his bony shoulder.

I asked one of the Marines, "What the fuck is that?"

"He's our local barber. For twenty-five cents he'll cut your hair. It's his rice bowl. He uses a comb and a straight razor."

"You guys trust that old fucker? You sit in that chair while he has a straight razor in his hand?"

"Fuckin' A! Don't worry about it. Just show him a coin, let him cut your hair, flip him a quarter."

"He don't work the other side of the bridge. The South Vietnamese fuck with him so he stays on this end. You watch him. Tomorrow he'll walk up and down this end of the bridge. He'll get a little business then we won't see him for two or three days."

I broke down and let him cut my hair. He didn't speak English and my Vietnamese was limited. It amounted to me pointing to my hair. He grunted, smiled, and bowed. The first time I was a little nervous. In truth, I was never able to completely relax while the old man worked on me.

It had been a good day—no one had died.

"Neither the sun nor death can be looked at with a steady eye." ~ Francois de La Rochefoucauld

6

"GET THAT BITCH"

*"Whatever makes a soldier sad will make a killer
smile." ~ The Captain, by Leonard Cohen*

GUNNY CALLED THE SQUAD LEADERS and fire team leaders
together. "We got us a Chou Hoi. He's gonna lead us to an
NVA camp in the mountains. Get your men to check their
gear. Tell 'em to shit-can everything they don't absolutely need.
It's gonna be a long walk—at least three, maybe four days. Okay,
that's all. Get it done."

I told the men in my fire team to be sure and fill their canteens,
check their ammo and grenades. Every man carried two bandoliers
of machine gun ammo. Two men in each fire team could carry an
extra mortar round in his pack. I passed out long-range rats which
met with a smile. We liked them a lot more than the regular C-rats.
You just heated up water and poured it into the bag, stirred or shook
the bag, added *Tabasco Sauce*, and chow was ready to eat.

Just as we were ready to leave Hill 88 and move out, a few of
the Marines jumped up and down, checking for anything loose that

might make noise or give us away. A deuce-and-a-half drove up the hill. The captain raised his arm, a signal for everyone to stop. Young women from the Red Cross piled out of the trucks.

All of a sudden, the strangest thing happened. Young men came out of the back of the trucks carrying musical instruments and sheet music.

The captain hollered out, "You men take a seat. These young ladies are going to pass out boxes for each of you. The band is going to entertain us. Keep your hands to yourself."

I asked other Marines who had been there longer than me if that had ever happened before.

"No fucking way."

"Isn't this loverly?"

They gave each of us a cold pop. In the white box we each got coffee, cigarettes, lifesavers, toilet paper, *Chiclets*, plug tobacco, sugar, and salt and pepper.

Dennis told me, "You keep those lifesavers on you, and you'll never die."

It sounded good, but just seeing those young girls running around lifted my spirits. The band played for about thirty minutes then loaded back into the trucks. We were still saddled up. It was too much trouble to take off those packs. As the trucks drove down the hill toward Route 1, we went the other direction toward the mountains.

We stopped in a small village in the late afternoon of the first day. A few Marines filled up their canteen from the villager's rain barrels. The captain wanted a bunch of us to gather around the Chu Hoi. He didn't want to chance someone recognizing him and warning the NVA camp. He wore Marine gear and pack but no weapon.

I filled up my canteen and pulled out a plug of *Day's Work*.

A young Vietnamese boy came running up, "Maline, Maline, chocolate, chocolate."

"No kid, this isn't chocolate."

"Maline, chocolate."

"Go ahead, Redus. Give the kid some chocolate."

I handed the plug to the kid. The look on his face when he bit down was priceless. He spit out what he bit off and threw the plug at me, turned, and ran off.

I can still see that kid. He had no shoes on, wore blue shorts and a white t-shirt. We laughed for a long time. Every once in a while, someone brought it up for a good laugh. The boy was probably five or six years old.

It was the last week of June, 1968. Just before we started climbing, the captain brought us together. He had something to say.

"From here on out, there will be no unnecessary talking—use hand signals. If you must talk, whisper. There will be no smoking until we come back out. We're going to take the long way around to the camp so we can come up behind them. Some of this trail is pretty steep so if you fall or bang your knee, keep your mouth shut. Bear the pain—you could give us away. Any questions? All right, Gunny take that first squad and lead us out."

It rained on us that first day in the mountains. The mud became slick as we pushed each other up that mountain. Stopping well before dark, we formed a circle with the captain, Gunny, Chu Hoi, and the staff sergeant in the middle.

Everybody carried C-4. We rolled it up a little ball about the size of a marble and lit it to heat water to pour in our long rats. After chow, we settled down for the night. Everybody in my fire team was within an arm's reach. Stevie then put out the claymore.

We were told not to put the claymore out any farther than we could see it. The gooks snuck up at night and would turn it around on us.

The claymore was an a-shaped charge with a backing of C-4. There were 900 steel balls at a sixty degree arc. It had a kill radius of one hundred yards.

The next morning, everyone was up and ready to move. I had coffee but no food. We would be at the NVA camp in a few hours. If we were lucky, we were going to catch them off guard. I'm sure they felt pretty safe there in the mountains. For some of them, it was going to be their last day on Earth.

About eleven o'clock, the point fire team spotted their camp. Gooks don't eat breakfast. They usually have their first meal of the day between eleven and twelve o'clock. The smoke from their cook fires hung in the treetops. They had no security out. We had caught them by surprise.

The captain split the unit into three parts, each with its own objective. One group would work their way around the camp and cover the bottom of the hill where the mountain stream ran down. The second group would cover the exit by the huge boulders, while my group would enter the camp through the mountain stream. There would be no escape. The signal to enter the camp was Dennis's job. He would fire a blooper round into the center of the camp. When it exploded, we were to go in.

Standing in that shallow mountain stream, the gooks were just a few feet away. They had no idea we were there. I was the fifth man from the front in a line waiting for the signal.

Boom!

The Marines in front of me pushed limbs out of the way, splashing as we ran to get into their camp. We moved quick so we would be on top of them before they knew what was happening.

As soon as the blooper round went off, it was followed by automatic weapons being fired. The Marines in front of me killed two VC next to the creek bank. As I passed by, there was rice scattered on the ground.

The VC on the left was sitting up, leaning against lattice work. The top of his head was gone. He still had both lips but after taking several rounds to his face, it was as if someone had chopped off everything above his upper lip. His head looked like a bowl. Everything in the bowl was red and gray.

I moved past him.

Moving past the second VC, he ,too, was sitting up, leaning against a rock wall. There were at least two rounds in his chest. I moved past him into the camp.

Slipping on a rock, I went down on my left knee but immediately stood back up firing my weapon. NVA ran everywhere, trying to escape. It was a kill box. They had nowhere to go. Some limped from being wounded. We showed them no mercy. I emptied one magazine, letting it fall into the creek. Putting a fresh magazine in, I fed a round into the chamber and continued to fire.

From the moment the blooper round set off the attack 'til the shooting stopped, it probably took a minute-and-a-half to two minutes. Then, it got quiet.

You could smell the cordite in the air. I never felt more alive.

Checking an NVA who was lying face down in the stream, blood ran out of him into the clear water and down the hill. Gunny stood next to me.

"You know, you could drink that water at the bottom of the hill. It will purify itself by the time it gets down there."

He no more than got the words out of his mouth, when a woman came running out of a small cave, made a dash across the stream—headed for the jungle.

Gunny hollered, "Get that bitch!"

I took off after her with Red, one of the machine gunners. For a moment we lost her but then suddenly there she was.

She stood about forty feet away next to large rocks, waving her arms, yelling, "No Maline, no Maline."

I told her, "*La Dai, La Dai.*" Vietnamese for come to me, come to me.

She just stood there waving her arms.

Red, carrying only a .45 stood off to my right. He leaned forward and suddenly began to fire. He told me later he caught a glimmer of a rifle barrel sticking out from behind a rock.

When Red fired his .45, the NVA moved. Red fired again. The NVA jumped when a couple of Red's rounds hit him. I saw the NVA clearly. As he fell forward, I fired.

Several of the rounds hit him, but the old woman was so close one of the rounds hit her below her ribcage on her left side. She spun back to her left and fell to the ground. Then, she jumped up and took off running. I knew I couldn't let her get away. If I couldn't catch her, I would have no choice. I had to drop her.

That old woman ran like a gazelle. I was loaded down with gear, trying to catch her. We probably ran another thirty to forty feet when I leaned out and grabbed her long hair, jerking her back. Her feet left the ground. She landed on her back. I quickly put my knee to her chest and grabbed her throat.

She tried to yell and spit out words.

I squeezed her throat harder, "Shut up! Shut up!"

Quickly looking around, I was afraid the noise she made might draw NVA to us. There were still rounds in my magazine, but I wasn't sure how many. I couldn't hold on to her and put in a fresh magazine. So, I got her to her feet. Hanging onto her clothes, we headed back to camp.

Gunny was piling up weapons and food. I noticed the bags of rice had writing on them, From the People of the United States of America with two hands clasping each other, one yellow and one white. In the tree line, I heard screaming and yelling. Some of the NVA were still alive.

I asked Gunny, "Are we gonna finish them off?"

"No, we're gonna blow these weapons and food and get the fuck outta here."

He looked at the old woman, "Take her down below the hill. A chopper is coming in to pick up her and another woman we found. They're going out with the wounded."

"Who got hit?"

"One of the machine gunners took a round in the foot."

Looking to my right, an NVA sat against a large rock. He had taken several rounds to his chest and one in his throat. Bloody froth bubbled from his mouth, pink in color.

Hanging on to the old woman, we worked our way down to the bottom of the hill. I saw a young girl standing there with a branch full of leaves over her head to shield her from the sun. As I got close to the young girl, I smelled something.

"What the hell is that smell?"

The Marines below the hill laughed, "It's her man. Too much boom, boom."

"Shit man, that's bad. And I thought I smelled."

"There's the chopper."

We were laughing. The crew in that chopper were going to have to smell her all the way to Da Nang.

The corpsman took care of the old woman. The hole was a through-and-through. No bones had been hit.

I saw the other Marines coming down the hill. We would be heading back to Freedom Bridge and then on to Hill 88.

It crossed my mind, *This is a war fought to the death.* There was no room for doubt or feelings when you pulled the trigger. Killing was easy. It was living with it that was hard.

The captain decided to set up an ambush below the NVA camp that night. He was hoping to catch NVA working their way up the hill.

Nothing came of it so after chow the next morning, we started the long walk back.

On the third night, we made camp again with the officers and NCOs in the center. The rest of the platoon made a circle around them. With everybody in my fire team within arm's reach, we split up the watch. Rations grew short, so we paired up—two men to one long range meal. With claymores out, we settled in for the night.

It was a good day. Nobody died.

One of the men in my fire team was having a rough time, especially at night. His nerves were becoming a problem. When it was his turn for watch, he kept waking me up.

Whispering in my ear he said, "There's something out there."

The two of us would sit and listen. It was so dark in the jungle you couldn't see more than a few feet in any direction. I sat there with him, listening.

When I was sure it was nothing, I whispered in his ear, "There's nothing out there."

Lying back down, I would just get back to sleep. He shook me again.

"There's something out there."

After sitting up the second time, I decided to stay up with him. It was easier on me. I would get some sleep after his watch.

That morning we grabbed chow, buried our trash, and made our way out of the mountains. A few of the Marines were beat down, so we took turns carrying their gear. When we finally broke into the open plain, I saw three trucks in the distance. They were driving on a muddy road, coming toward us. It was the Navy bringing us hot chow.

The captain had us gather around. "I want one fire team from each squad for security. You squad leaders will replace the men on watch after your men have eaten. The Navy has brought paper plates, cups, and utensils so you won't need your gear. Now go. Get in line."

With that, we broke up and headed for the chow line. The captain and the two sergeants were the last to eat. They waited until their men had been fed.

Lying on the ground, using my flak jacket for a pillow with my belly full, I heard something. Sitting up, I saw a chopper coming in.

I asked a Marine, "What's up?"

He pointed off to the left to a Marine kneeling beneath a tree. I immediately recognized him. He was one of the men in my fire team. He was the same Marine I had stayed up with during his last watch. Once the Huey landed, he ran, bent over for the chopper. Just a few feet from the door he fell, then crawled to the helicopter where a Marine pulled him on board. Seconds later he was gone.

I went looking for Doc. The corpsman would know what just happened.

"Doc, how come they picked up that Marine? He's in my fire team. No one said a word to me."

"He's had it, so I called in a medevac. They'll deal with it in Da Nang."

Maybe I could have done more, tried to help him in some way. But we all have our own demons. I had to keep my eye on him. He was losing his nerve. When we hit that NVA camp, he saw the killing that went on, the bodies lying everywhere. It was too much for him. He broke. Had he stayed he might have locked up, putting not only his life on the line but the lives of other Marines in the unit.

Being on watch in the jungle at night played havoc on your nerves. When darkness came, you could only see a few feet. With the rain falling, it was hard to see or hear anything. Lightning messed not only with your night vision, but you started seeing things—movement that wasn't really there. Or was it?

I think my worst nights were sitting there when there was sudden movement.

After a few nerve-wracking moments, I realized it was only a small animal moving around.

My heart beat faster. I strained to pick up the noise again as it moved away.

The men in my fire team needed their sleep. If I did see a gook, he would be close. The sound of my weapon would rouse them.

Making it back to Freedom Bridge, the guys were worn out. The captain made arrangement for trucks to haul the Marines back to the hill. I decided to stay behind and wash up in the creek. Another Marine, Jake thought it sounded like a good idea, so the two of us broke down to our pants. Neither of us had any soap but it felt good to rinse off.

After a few minutes, Jake decided to get dressed and head back. I told him I would be along. There was always traffic on the road. All I had to do was raise my arm and a trucker would stop for me.

I finally figured I had done enough. The blood on my pants was still there but the blood under my fingernails was just about gone. Grabbing my clothes and boots, I air dried, threw my pack on my back, picked up my weapon, and headed for the road. It didn't take long to hail a ride.

I thanked the driver and started up the hill. Just as I was about halfway up, I heard a loud explosion. Running up the road, a jeep driving fast and erratic, headed right for me. Gunny rode shotgun. They stopped.

"Don't go up there. There's mines."

He drove off. I continued up the hill. What I saw were several Marines standing around a body on the ground. About twenty feet away lay another body and a Marine in tears.

"What the hell happened?"

"Jake came walking up the hill and stepped on what we think was a box mine. A piece of shrapnel flew across the hill striking Boxer in the chest. At first, we thought he was just wounded. It knocked him backwards off that log. He sat up and said, 'I'll be damned. My first purple heart.' Then he just slumped over. We grabbed him and tried to sit him up. He was dead."

A piece of shrapnel had pierced his heart. I walked back over to the Marine who had stepped on the mine. The blast had broken every bone in his body. I couldn't recognize him. The mine caused immediate death. He had felt no pain.

"Are you sure this is Jake? We were just down at the bridge rinsing off."

"Yeah man, it's Jake."

One of the other Marines brought over a body bag. When we tried to pick up Jake, he fell apart in our hands. It was no use. We couldn't pick him up.

A Marine brought a stretcher and laid it beside the body. With four of us on one side and four on the other side, we dug into the dirt beneath the body with our fingers. We pushed while the other four Marines tried to lift him just enough so we could push him onto the stretcher. It worked. We got him on the stretcher and covered his body. We had questions.

"How could this happen?"

"Aren't the engineers supposed to check this fucking hill for mines and booby-traps before we come back?"

"The captain told us the hill was checked. He said box mines are hard to detect."

We loaded the two dead Marines in the back of a jeep. Someone would take them to Phu Bai. At times, I felt like death was out there watching me, smiling. All I could do was smile back.

Jake, one of the two Marines killed on the hill sat next to me on the bleachers at Pendleton that rainy morning when the Marine officer told us, "When you go home, do everything you want to do. Some of you are not coming back."

The next day my squad was moving down the road to Freedom Bridge. *Maybe someone will have a bar of soap.*

* * *

Just as I was finishing up with chow, Dennis walked up.

"The captain just passed the word. Two squads are going out tonight. We're gonna work our way along the railroad upgrade, go through that big culvert pipe, cross the paddies and set up in the tree line. He got intel the gooks are gonna hit Freedom Bridge tonight. We're gonna be the blocking force. The South Vietnamese are being filled-in right now. They'll be putting men out on their end. I'll see you in about thirty minutes after I eat something and check my gear."

As darkness closed in over us, we moved out. The night was clear. There was no moon but there were no clouds either. Moving along and below the upgrade, I made my way to the large culvert pipe. It was big enough for villagers to move their water buffalo through it to the paddies on the other side.

My fire team was on point. Using hand signals, we crawled through the large culvert. There was plenty of room to stand up. But if the NVA were waiting on us, all they had to do was fire through that hole on the other end.

Moving through the mud, we were about halfway through when suddenly, CRACK, CRACK, CRACK. Lying as flat as possible, my eyes were fixed on the opening. Rounds were ricocheting off concrete walls. I was watching for a ChiCom to come flying into the pipe. Just then, I started to feel sick. For most of the day my stomach was upset. The next thing I knew I was having the dry heaves. Doc was suddenly lying in the mud next to me.

"Redus, are you hit? Are you hit?"

"No, Doc. I'm sick."

"The captain wants you and your men outta the pipe."

"Right, Doc. Fuck!"

I grabbed my men, whispering to them. "Come on, let's go. Let's get the fuck outta here."

Once we were out of the pipe, Gunny told me to move along the upgrade toward the bridge. At some point we would crawl up and over the top. After about eighty to one hundred yards, my Marines climbed up the steep grade. Just as I got to the top, star shells went off above us. They turned night into day.

Lying down on the railroad tracks, I heard the captain below me, in a loud whisper, "Stop firing those God-damn flares. Cease fire. Cease fire. I've got men out here!"

After what seemed longer than it probably was, it got dark again. We crossed the paddies and made our way to the tree line, but no contact was made.

When daylight came, we made our way back to the bridge. Doc grabbed me. We commandeered a jeep and headed for Phu Bai. After dropping off our gear, we headed for the medical shack.

They drew blood and gave me the bad news. I had amoeba poisoning probably from drinking bad water. The doctor came in with a metal syringe that looked to be about eight inches long. The plunger also was metal and had a ring at the end to put your finger through. The needle looked way too long. He headed toward me and smiled.

"Marine, this is the worst shot you will ever take. Drop your pants, put your left arm on the corpsman's shoulder, and let you left leg hang loose. Are you ready?"

"Yes, sir."

He stuck that needle into my left cheek. He was right. It hurt some kind of bad.

"Doc! Doc!"

"Hang on, Marine. I'm just about done. Hang on. There, it's over with."

I limped around for a few steps as I pulled up my pants.

"Now, I want you to go out and walk around for about thirty minutes."

"Aye-aye, sir."

Doc and I walked back to our area.

"Get some chow and some sleep. We'll leave for the bridge in the morning."

"Thanks, Doc. To hell with chow. I'm going to find me an empty bunk and sleep 'til morning."

7

HE KILLED A KID LAST NIGHT

"I believe that each person is more than the worst thing they've ever done." ~ Bryan Stevenson

IN EARLY JULY 1968, MY platoon was ordered to An Hoi for a few days to patrol and to man the wire at the edge of the perimeter. There were small concrete block houses about seven feet off the ground with layers of sandbags on top every thirty yards. We climbed on top, three to a block house and took turns on watch while the other two slept.

It was the first time I ever used a starlight scope. Looking through it, everything was green and black. It surprised me how clear and distinct the sight picture was looking out past the four lines of razor wire and into the brush.

The dark had no secrets. There was no contact.

The next day I ate lunch in the chow hall. It was always a good thing to get a hot meal. When I got my tray full and looked for a table, I was surprised to see an old friend.

James Quinn and I had gone through boot camp together at MCRD. The talk spread from stories about our platoon, the sergeants, and the individuals we had spent those nine weeks with. He told me about a hot LZ he had just been pulled out of that morning.

I noticed a Marine off to the right, he was sobbing. I asked Quinn if he knew what was going on.

"He killed a kid last night in an ambush."

"I recognize him. Wasn't he in our platoon in boot camp?"

"Yeah, he was in my squad. He's been like that all morning."

"I'm gonna go talk to him."

"It won't do any good."

"I'll be right back."

As I sat across from the sobbing Marine, I asked him, "Hey man, do you remember me?"

He nodded.

"I heard what happened. It's nobody's fault. It's tough about the kid, but you and I both know the gooks use villagers and kids to haul their gear. In an ambush you don't have time to pick and choose your targets."

"I know but he was a kid. And I killed him."

"It's tough, I know but you can't blame yourself." I took his hand and squeezed it. "Hang in there. You'll get through this."

Standing up, I went back to the table with Quinn.

"He's in a world of shit but he's gonna have to get it together."

"I hope he makes it."

We finished our meal, shook hands. Once outside the chow hall we went our separate ways.

That night I was on the wire again. Nothing happened either night, but the third day would be seared into my brain.

It was mid-afternoon. The platoon was spread out on a partial blacktop road outside An Hoi. I thought it looked strange as I looked to my right. There were three partially burned down houses sitting on large lots. They looked like houses you would see in any city back in the states. They seemed out of place.

Moving down the road a short time later, I heard the CRACK, CRACK of small arms fire. As I checked my weapon, Gunny came running up.

"Get ready. They are getting the shit kicked out of them. They are pulling out. We're going in!"

As Gunny moved past me, he continued barking at Marines on down the road. Just then up ahead, an APC (armored personnel carrier) drove up the road toward us. The driver got to me and turned to my right into a dry ditch. In the back of the APC, the gate was down. On top of the gate, bodies of dead Marines were stacked like cord wood with their boots facing me. I tried several times to count the number of bodies, but I kept losing count. It all happened in a short space of time.

I heard Gunny's voice, "Move up. Let's go. Get in line."

I checked my weapon again as we moved off the road into the jungle. Getting those dead Marines' bodies out of my mind wasn't easy.

I kept telling myself, "Put it away. Put it away."

We moved into the jungle, maybe 150 to 200 yards. There was no contact. The gooks had melted into the jungle again. When we pulled back to the road, the APC was gone.

Making our way back to An Hoi the next day, trucks took us out to Phu Loc 6. It was going to be our new home. The captain told everybody no more soft covers. "There are a lot of booby-traps in the area. Wear your helmets."

We filled sandbags, cleaned out trenches, and strung wire. One Marine heated up water for coffee.

"Hey, have any of you guys got a clean sock? I need one to use as a strainer."

A Marine threw him a sock. After putting in the coffee, he tied a knot in the end.

"Give me a few minutes. You get the first cup."

Several of us got our cups. It smelled like the coffee was ready. As we gathered around, Jackie poured each of us a cup. Sipping the hot coffee, we started to look at each other. It looked like coffee. It smelled like coffee. It tasted funny.

"Whose sock was that?"

"Dennis, was that a clean sock?"

"It sure looked clean to me. I rinsed my socks in the creek at Freedom Bridge before we left. That's the best you're gonna get. There's not an SOB on this hill that's got a new sock. So, cut out the bitching, drink your coffee. Does anyone need sugar?"

We had a good laugh. It felt good for a few minutes—we were somewhere else.

* * *

Riley got in touch with me. The squad was going out about ten hundred hours. We'd be gone most of the day working our way through the village, across the paddies, towards the countryside and the tree line.

On that particular day, the sun felt warmer than usual. The fog was burned off, but the humidity was high. There was no sense in getting worked up over the humidity. It wouldn't change anything.

As we neared the tree line, shots suddenly rang out. We were still in high grass and brush. I was a good fifty to sixty yards from the tree line. Hitting the deck, I rolled over on my back pointing my weapon toward the jungle, in case the gooks decided to come out. A Marine ahead of me wasn't moving so I hit his boot with my fist.

"Move, motherfucker! Move!"

Just as soon as those words left my mouth, I knew it was a mistake. The gooks heard me.

They shoot at movement and sound. As the gook emptied a full magazine, the rounds went across my chest as I lie there. Off to my left was a small bush about three feet tall. As the rounds flew across my chest, that bush was literally sheared off. Pieces of limb and leaves flew through the air. Had he lowered his weapon just one inch when he fired, the gook's rounds would have hit me, cutting me in two.

I said nothing else.

The Marine in front of me was locked up. He hadn't moved so I stayed low and worked my way past him until I got to cover. Working my way into the tree line, I found cover and got to one knee, returning fire. The thought crossed my mind there was no sound like a round hitting the tree you're hiding behind. Splinters and pieces of wood flew in the air.

The AK put a lot of rounds down range but it was not as accurate as the M-16.

After what seemed like an eternity, the gooks cut it off and melted back into the jungle. They usually hit quick and hard, then broke it off.

During a firefight, a second seemed like a minute. A minute felt like an hour. An hour or more seemed like Hell. In that firefight, after we counted noses nobody had taken a hit. It surprised me with the rounds flying around. It was a miracle—one of God's footsteps.

A few days later, Marines brought in a couple of dead VC. Both of them were tied to long poles of bamboo. It reminded me of the pictures I had seen of natives in Africa hauling an animal they had killed into camp.

Back at Freedom Bridge, a squad of South Vietnamese brought in two VC the same way. I walked over for a look when this South Vietnamese officer pulled out a knife and cut off the left ear of one of the VC. He then looked at me and put the ear in his mouth, biting down.

"Is that all you got?"

He promptly cut off the other ear and walked off. I had seen Marines with a necklace of ears around their neck hanging from a shoelace. The dried-out ears turned a golden brown over time and got as hard as a buckle.

They hung the VC upside down by their feet between three bamboo poles, a tripod, one at each end of the bridge. One of the Marines told me it was a warning to the gooks.

"If we catch you, this is what we're gonna do to you."

Staff Sgt. Phelps told me it was a dirty war.

8

"REDUS IS DEAD"

"It is well that war is so terrible, otherwise we should grow too fond of it." ~ Robert E. Lee

JUST BEFORE DARK, RILEY CAME walking over. "I want you and Mitchell to be on LP tonight."

"You got to be shitting me. He's new. Why not Joey or Tobi?"

"Look, I know he's new. He needs the experience. We're short-handed so cut out the bitching. Just get it done."

"Yeah."

I told Mitchell to meet me at the wire after dark. Then, I approached the machine gunners. It was important to let them know exactly where we were gonna set in for the night. If they saw one of us move, I didn't want them to open up on us.

Mitch met me at the wire.

"Look, I know this is new to you. Usually there're three of us out there. Riley is shorthanded, so it's gonna be you and me. We'll sit back-to-back—no talking. We'll set in just the other side of that tree. If you hear or see anything, get my attention. Now here's the bad news. I don't know you so we're going to have to stay awake all night. If I feel you slumping over, I'll shake you. They're going to key our mic on the radio once every hour. All we do is key it back. That way they'll know we're still alive and awake. One more thing, if we make contact, getting back up the hill we're on our own. Any questions?"

He shook his head, "No."

We made our way past the wire. It was dark and cloudy. Thank God, there was no moon.

As the hours passed, I had my usual hallucinations. I could swear that brush just moved or it looked like something was moving from tree to tree, but it was nothing. I bit my lip, stretched, hummed a song in my brain, whatever it took to stay awake.

There were nights when it rained and then you really started seeing things that weren't there. In the rain there was lightning. Lightning really made it hard to see at night.

The night went without incident. A heavy fog hung around the trees. As the sun began to rise, beams of light broke through the canopy. The radio suddenly came to life.

"Get up here. The gooks are in the village."

"We're on our way."

Mitch and I stood up, took a quick look around, and headed for the hill. Once on top, Marines were running down the road.

Riley hollered at me, "Take your fire team out on the road. Once we get close to the village, take your men into the jungle. Enter it from this side. Another squad will enter from the road. Dennis has another fire team. They'll enter from the jungle. Come up on the backside. Got it?"

"You bet."

As I came out of the jungle, the fire team in front of me led the way. As I stepped into the clearing, I felt something was wrong. The village was deserted. Again, checking my weapon, making sure it was on full auto and the safety was off, I followed the Marines in front of me. Then the silence was broken.

I heard CRACK, CRACK, CRACK as rounds screamed by me.

The AK is a formidable weapon. It's not as accurate as the M-16 but can put a lot of rounds down range. The weapon fires a 7.62 mm high velocity bullet that makes a distinct sound.

Several Marines carried AKs in the company. Even though the captain discouraged it, he never said no. In a firefight, it was hard to see the enemy at times, so you shot at movement or sound. If you heard the AK going off to your right, in the chaos you might have thought the NVA were trying to flank us. If we couldn't see the Marines, some might have starting putting rounds on them.

As we moved across the embankment, in milliseconds men dove into the rice paddy looking for cover. The Marine about eight to ten feet in front of me started to move then staggered, making it to the paddy. He turned and fell backward into the water.

I made it to the embankment, hugging it, and tried to stay as low as possible with the lower part of my body in the water. As I hugged the dirt wall, the gooks put several rounds around the body of the Marine, now lying motionless.

They were trying to draw one of us out by thinking he was still alive. They hoped one of us would run out, grab the wounded Marine, and pull him to the embankment. It was a kill box. It was suicide.

The Marine was just a few feet away. If I leaned out, maybe I could grab him by the boot and pull him to me.

As I leaned forward, a round went right by my ear. It was so close. I was sure the sniper had nicked me. I jumped back against the wall of dirt.

"You fucker. You motherfucker." Running my hand against my ear, there was no blood.

I was sure the sniper was on the ground. He was shooting across at me, putting rounds in the dirt above my head. Had he been in a tree, he would have had the angle for a kill. He would have been shooting down on me. That was good news. I could ease my body into the paddy, grab the Marine's right boot with both my boots, and pull him to me.

I kept talking to him, repeating myself.

"Hang on. Hang on. I've got you. I've got you."

It was slow at first but I was finally able to pull him close. While trying to stay low and with one final jerk, I pulled him up next to me.

His eyes were set. His mouth was full of paddy water. He was dead. He had taken a round through his heart.

Later, I remembered that dead Marine had been in Vietnam two weeks longer than I had.

Other Marines flanked the snipers. We searched for bloody trails or drag marks hoping we had brought death to them—hoping to exact revenge. We found nothing.

I remember reading a line from an English officer during the war with Napoleon. "Throw the dice, and we shall match death throw for throw."

We put the dead Marine in a body bag and placed him in the back of a jeep. It always came back to me each time I did it.

He's dead. I know it. His family will find out in a few days when a Marine will knock on their door. I did my best to try and save him.

What I didn't know was the young Marine was dead within a few seconds after the round entered his chest.

Another Marine died that morning, along with three wounded. I didn't know it at the time but in a couple of hours, I, too, would have my brush with death.

"A son is a man's immortality."

Death had become a big part of my life. It was something you had to overcome. There were no guarantees in war. Either you climb out of the mud or you die.

Whenever I checked the enemy to see if he was dead, a Marine kept his weapon on him while I turned him over. Sticking your finger in his eye was a good way to be sure, if it's not obvious from his wounds.

"When you kill a man, you take away everything he has, everything he would have had."

It seemed to me that whether it was a Marine or a gook, the dead seemed to have a look of surprise on their face. It was as if to say, "I didn't expect this to happen to me." Or their eyes simply stared at me. No matter if I was standing in front or to the side, their eyes followed me. Sometimes the dead would have a lazy eye. The eyelids would be half open. Whatever the case, as I put the Marine into a body bag my last thought was, "I hope he didn't suffer."

After the firefight was over, the all-clear was given. I took a deep breath. I smelled the cordite in the air. I never felt more alive.

We made our way back to Phu Loc 6. I got word the mine sweepers needed cover on their flanks as they checked the road between our hill and the Alamo—a village we nicknamed not far from us. The staff sergeant told me to take my fire team and walk the right flank to keep the engineers from being ambushed.

When we neared the village, Staff yelled, "Put your men on that hill. I don't want the gooks looking down on us!"

"Yes, sir."

With three men in my fire team, I placed two on the opposite side. "You, down there. You, over here. Keep your eyes open. Mouse, you come with me!"

As Mouse and I walked along the crest, I decided to put him on that side. I would take up a position further down.

There was a trail. I had walked it once already. It was clear but for some reason, I took a shorter route. It was a mistake. The trail wound around like a horseshoe. Instead of staying on the trail, I crossed over. The gooks knew Americans like to take shortcuts. I had been told many times, "Don't do it."

Where my mind was, I couldn't say. You couldn't make mistakes out here. Mistakes got you killed. Maybe it was because I hadn't slept but four hours in three days. Perhaps, I was still thinking about the ambush that morning. In any case, I hadn't put it aside yet. I was about to make a mistake that could cost both of our lives.

As I moved through short grass, my left boot got hung up. When I felt the tug on my boot, I remember thinking, "Please God, let that be a stick."

Looking down I saw a com wire across my left boot. Following the wire to my left, I saw it was attached to a Chi Com grenade. I didn't panic. Anyone who has ever been in a tight spot will tell you your brain works in milliseconds as long as you don't panic. The Chi Com doesn't have the killing power of an American grenade. There was a good chance Mouse and I could both come out of it alive.

I quickly turned to my left and hollered, "Run, Mouse. It's a booby-trap."

As I turned to throw myself on the ground, the lights went out. I never heard the explosion. As I came to, I heard a voice that sounded a long way off.

"Redus is dead!"

As I lie there, I had no feeling in my body. Everything was black. I couldn't see. At first I thought, *If this is death, it's not bad.* Then, I heard the voice again but closer.

"Redus is dead!"

I began repeating over and over in my mind, *I'm not gonna die. I'm not gonna die.* I felt my body being lifted up by someone. My sight was coming back. It was Doc, our corpsman. My body was tingling.

It reminded me of when I was a kid. A firecracker had gone off in my hand.

My whole body stung and tingled. As I sat up, I reached for my legs, running my hands up my body. I checked my biscuits, both arms, and my chest. When I reached for my head, Doc grabbed my wrist.

"Don't touch your head. You're hit in the head!"

"How bad is it Doc?"

"I called for Emergency Evacuation."

I knew what that meant—get here quick or he is going to die. I stayed calm.

There were times when I saw other Marines lose it. Their hearts beat faster. They lost a lot of blood, went into shock and died. There was a promise I had made to myself. If I took a hit, no matter how bad it was, no matter the pain, I would bear it. I would fight for my life.

Doc told me, "I can't give you anything for pain cause it's a head wound. You need to stay alert."

"That's all right, Doc. I'm not hurting that bad."

"How's Mouse? Did he make it?"

"See for yourself."

As I looked past my boots about six feet away, there was Mouse. He was on his stomach on the ground propped up on his elbows.

He had a cigarette in his mouth and a big smile on his face as our eyes met each other.

When I had yelled to him, he'd had time to turn around. Shrapnel had hit him in both legs. He was alive.

A couple of Marines and the Doc helped me get to my feet. They took off my gear. I had two bandoliers of machine gun ammo over my flak jacket, four grenades, twenty magazines of M-16 ammo, and a bandolier of M-16 ammo. None of it went off in the explosion.

They took my two canteens as Doc finished wrapping my head. I started to walk down the hill as a CH-46 was about to land on the dirt road below. The two Marines offered to carry me instead, so I agreed. My head felt a little woozy.

As we started down, after only a few steps they fell. We went to the ground. Getting up to try again, we went a few more steps and they fell again. The hill *was* steep, but I decided to walk on my own.

"You guys are gonna kill me!"

When the Marines below the hill heard me, they broke out laughing and yelling. As I moved down the hill, I stopped, looking at the Marines with their arms up covering their eyes from the wind and dust from the chopper's two props. The wheels of the helicopter were coming off the ground a good foot, with the props wound up tight ready to take off at a moment's notice.

Just then the crew chief hollered at me, "Come on, we gotta get off the ground."

I was the last to board. The three Marines wounded that morning at the village plus Mouse were sitting and standing up forward in the cabin behind the two pilots. Working my way to them, the men on both the port and starboard side manned machine guns with US Air force printed on the back of their white helmets. None of us said a word. The flight took about fifteen minutes for us to land at the Naval Hospital in Da Nang.

Once the chopper landed, I walked out under my own power. Several people passed me, two with a stretcher heading for the helicopter to help the Marines who were unable to walk out on their own. Two corpsmen grabbed me by my arms and led me to a wooden table about four feet off the ground. They laid me down and cut my clothes off of me while one went through my pockets.

The nurse told me to lay back and take a deep breath, but I sat up.

"I want that medallion!"

"Lie back Marine and breathe deep."

The nurse was very insistent but somehow through it all, I remembered the Marine *Globe and Anchor* Mr. Gardner had given to me the last time I was home. It was made of lead and had taken a beating in the right pocket of my jungle utilities. I considered it my good luck charm. I wasn't going to let them put me under until I had it in my hand.

"Here Marine, is this what you wanted?"

I took it from him, closed my hand, and held it.

"Now give it back. I'll put it in this small paper sack. You'll get it back later after recovery. Okay?"

Sometimes life is like trying to suck honey off of a thorn.

I handed it back to him, leaned back, took a deep breath, and the lights went out.

When I came to in the hospital, someone was slapping my right hand. Opening my eyes and looking to my right, a Vietnamese nun—wings and all—was yelling at me.

"Wake up, Corporal Weedus. Wake up, Corporal Weedus. Doctor. *Doctor!*"

I had several pillows behind my head, so I was kind of sitting up. As I gazed around the room, I looked down. I was as naked as the day I was born. There was a pee tube on my willy, and my head was wrapped. Other than that—nothing.

Hearing voices, I looked up. There, on a TV hanging from the ceiling was Hoss and Joe Cartwright. *Bonanza* was on. I found out later tapes of popular shows were sent over from the States.

The nun continued slapping my hand, hollering for the doctor. I glanced at her and passed out.

When I later came to, I had been covered with a sheet. A nurse walked toward me.

"How are you feeling?"

"My head hurts a little. How long have I been out?"

"This is your second day. You slept a long time. The doctor will be here shortly. He'll answer your questions. Would you like some *Jell-o*?"

"You bet I would."

It didn't take long. The doctor showed up before the *Jell-o*.

"Good afternoon, my name is Dr. La Monte."

"Hello, Doc. How bad is it?"

"You're an extremely lucky young man. With a head wound of this sort, shall we say, magnitude, you're extremely lucky to be alive. The fact you have no motor problems, you can walk, move your arms is incredible.

"I left two pieces of shrapnel in your brain. They were both so deep I felt that if I went after them, I possibly would make you a vegetable. Don't concern yourself—your body will form a protective barrier over them. They will stay right where they are. They won't move.

"As you've probably noticed, we have taken out the tubes in your body. If you need to go to the head, get a corpsman to help you. Now, do you have any questions?"

"No, Doc, you've answered about everything I can think of."

"There is one more thing I have to say. I had to remove a piece of your brain about the size of a plum. You've lost an area of your skull about two inches square. At some point they will probably put a plate in your head but that's months away. I was somewhat hesitant to bring this up now, but you seem to be handling this very well."

"One question, Doc. Will I be able to play ball again?"

"I would say you have about a fifty-fifty chance."

"Thanks, Doc."

He walked away. My *Jell-o* showed up. I watched TV, then the nurse gave me several shots in my hip.

It became a little game between us. Back then syringes were made of glass. I could hear her coming as she pushed a metal cart full of syringes. They banged against each other, making a tinkling sound.

She leaned over telling me, "Corporal, I know you're not asleep so turn over. Which hip do you want to get your shots in?"

"Yes, ma'am. How about my right cheek today? My rear is black and blue from the shots I've had to take."

On my second day in the hospital, I woke up to three Marines standing at the end of my bed. There was nobody I wanted to see more. It lifted my spirits. They told me Golf Company was moving closer to Da Nang so they asked the CO for permission. They got a ride in a passing truck, grabbed chow at the mess hall, and came by to see how I was making out.

A cloud hung over me when they left. I felt guilty that somehow I had let them down. They were shorthanded. To put into words how I felt when I saw them leave would be impossible. I just didn't have the words.

On the third day when the doctor showed up, I asked him if I could go outside, breathe fresh air, and feel the sun on my face. He told me he didn't think I was strong enough yet, but if I decided not to heed his advice I should take a corpsman with me.

After things slowed down, one of the corpsmen agreed to go outside with me.

There was a bench just outside the Quonset hut. As I sat there feeling the sun on my face something happened. I felt a little lightheaded.

"Doc! Doc. I don't think I'm gonna make it!"

The corpsman got to me just as I passed out. The next thing I remember was waking up in my bed with my doctor standing over me.

"I tried to tell you. You're just not strong enough yet."

"Yes, sir. Doc, you were right. I just wanted to feel the sun."

There were no more attempts to go outside until the early morning hours of my fourth day. The nurse woke me.

"Corporal Redus, you need to get on the stretcher. The corpsman will help you with your robe. We're flying you to Japan."

They carried me out to an ambulance then to the flight line. We were boarding a C-141 Starlifter just like the one I flew on from El Toro to the Philippines back in 1967. There were ambulatory patients in the seats while those of us on stretcher were hung along the belly of the plane about three feet high.

I asked one of the nurses, "Why are they taking us out at three o'clock in the morning?"

"They don't want the enemy to know how many wounded we're taking out."

A lot of Vietnamese worked at the base during the day. They were screened but some were bound to be VC or NVA sympathizers.

The flight didn't seem long. When I woke up, they were moving me to 249th Army General Hospital just outside of Tokyo.

9

249TH ARMY GENERAL HOSPITAL

"I believe that man will not merely endure: he will prevail." ~ William Faulkner

WHEN WE LANDED AT THE air base, there were several ambulances waiting to take me and the other non-ambulatory young men to the hospital. Entering our room, it was long and narrow with eight beds on each side.

The first person I talked to was a Navy corpsman in the bed next to me. He had taken a round in the stomach. He pulled up his pajama top and showed me the shit sack that was attached to his body. There was no bitterness in the way he talked. He was glad to be alive.

As the weeks went by, I would have an opportunity to talk to everyone at one time or another. They all, to a man, were grateful to be spared.

The second night I was there, I became restless. I couldn't sleep. It finally came to me I was used to sleeping on the ground. The bed was too soft. Leaving my pillow on the bed, I crawled down to the floor. In a few minutes, I was asleep.

During the night, the duty nurse came by making a bed check. That was to check to make sure we were counted and to see to any needs we might have. When she turned her flashlight on my bunk, I was gone.

She immediately stepped between the beds and tripped and fell on top of me. We had a bit of a tussle, causing other nurses to come to her aid and waking everyone in the ward. The lights came on.

"Corporal, what do you think you are doing down there?"

"Ma'am, I'm used to sleeping on the ground. That mattress is too soft. I can't go to sleep."

"You can get back in that bunk, now. Tomorrow we will find you a mattress that is not so soft."

"Yes, ma'am."

As I crawled back in my bunk, everyone was awake. Some of the guys had a good laugh. The others just had big smiles.

For several days the guys kept asking, "What was it like when that nurse landed on you?"

I repeatedly told them the same thing—for a few seconds it was touch and go.

When I first felt her on me, I instinctively grabbed her by the throat but at that same instance, I realized who she was. I let her go. She had a smell about her and then I saw her officer bars. I came to my senses and tried to help her up. Her cover was off to the side a little but other than that I don't think she was hurt.

The next morning, a couple of Army guys brought me a sheet of plywood and a mattress that was all of two inches thick. I thanked the nurses. For the thirty days until I left for the States, I slept in my bunk.

We had the run of the base with our robes and pajamas on. We could take in a movie, go to chow, watch TV, or just walk around.

The corpsman next to me left for the States. In his place was an enlisted Army man with a busted leg. Using a wheelchair, I pushed him all over the base. He never spoke of his wound, and I never asked—not wanting to pry. I figured when he got ready to tell me about it, it would be a good time to be a good listener.

One afternoon, a bunch of us pulled our beds together. We were to each tell their own story and talk about how we were wounded. The guy in the wheelchair also pushed his bed towards the circle.

It was his turn to talk.

"My name is Sig. I was stationed in Camron Bay. My job was to draw maps for a general. One day I was playing basketball, I fell and broke my leg."

It got real quiet. All those young men had serious wounds from combat. One young man was in a partial body cast. Not a word was spoken for probably ten seconds, then someone snickered. Then someone else laughed. Then we all laughed.

Sig had given us the best medicine we could get—laughter.

Nobody gave him a hard time. He was one of us. I had been pushing him around the base for a week, and he never said a word. Sig was a breath of fresh air. He could have lied about his wound. We would have never known the difference, but he told the truth. I was lucky to have met him. Sig Hall was a man of character.

As the weeks went by, Sig was on his way back to the States. The doctor in Da Nang had used wire stitches to close my scalp. He told me normal stitches would not be strong enough. The day Sig left, I got my stitches out. They used a wire cutter.

When he cut the stitches (I think there were fourteen), the doctor knew it was painful for me. It hurt like hell.

There had been several times in my life when I needed stitches, but I don't remember it ever hurting like it did that morning. Hell, when the grenade hit me and I was coming to, my head didn't hurt as bad as it did the morning Doc came in with his wire cutter.

After the nurse cleaned my scalp where the stitches had been, she gave me a shot to help with the pain. After a few more days and a few more shots, the pain was gone. My hair was growing out. The rumor was I would be going back to the States in another week or so.

I was getting used to the routine, but nobody had taken Sig's old bed.

One morning I had just gotten back from breakfast when I noticed several new faces—one young man, just across from me and a couple of beds to the left. Another was sitting up in his bed and sobbing.

I asked, "Why is that guy over there crying?"

"They're sending him back."

"You would think if he made it to Japan his wounds would be bad enough to send him home."

"Fuckin' A! I don't know man. I don't know."

I thought about going over and talking to him but decided against it. If, in fact, they were sending him back, nothing I could say would make any difference. The Marine in the chow hall at An Hoi who cried over a kid he had killed was brought back to mind.

That I could talk to him but not this kid in the bed across from me about going back to Vietnam? I just didn't know what to say.

It was the last week in August, 1968. I had been there almost a month. I had gained weight and my head had healed up nicely. There was a new man in the bunk next to me. He was in the civil service and was recuperating from surgery.

After a couple of days, he was up and walking around. There was a Japanese girl in his life, and he wanted me to go on a picnic with them.

I told him, "There's no way they're gonna let me out of here to go on a picnic."

"Look, it's easy. She's going to come and pick me up. We'll drive around to the back and pick you up. You lie down in the floorboard. I'll throw a blanket over you. We drive through the gate and head into Tokyo. They don't ever stop me at the gate. They just salute me. I've got a sticker on my bumper for the Civil Service. There's this beautiful park we go to. You'll love it."

"What about your friend? Maybe she doesn't want any company."

"I called her this morning. She's fine with it. Come on, wouldn't you like to get out of here for a few hours? They'll never miss you. Hell, they won't even know you're gone. What do you say?"

"What time do I meet you out back?"

"Eleven-thirty."

"Count me in."

At 11:30 in robe and pajamas, I slowly walked out the door and headed for the back of the hospital. They were sitting there waiting for me. He introduced me to his girlfriend.

I got down on the floorboard and covered up as she drove toward the gate.

"Be real still and don't say a word."

Once we were well past the gate, he told me I could sit up. As I sat there, I never said a word.

Tokyo was a beautiful city. It was so clean. When we got to the park, I stepped out of the car and took a deep breath. God, it felt good to be alive. The park was beautiful. Everything was so green. There was a small stream below us. Tokyo and Mount Fuji were spread out in front of me. It was one of those *God's footsteps* moments.

The meal was great. I didn't talk much. I walked off by myself. They were nice enough to invite me. There was no need to intrude on their privacy. A long walk seemed like a good idea.

Watching the water in the stream, I heard him yell it was time to go back. When we got to within eyesight of the base gate, I laid down in the floorboard and covered up. She pulled around the back and let me out. After thanking them both for a wonderful afternoon, I went back into the hospital. No one had missed me.

Doc told me I was flying out the next day. We flew from Japan to Alaska then to the Marine Air Station at Millington, Tennessee just outside Memphis.

A Marine liaison stopped by a week before to present my Purple Heart to me. The day before I left, he stopped by to give me a uniform to wear on my trip back to the States.

"Can I see your Purple Heart again?"

"Sure, you bet."

"Oh look, there's a piece of dirt in here!"

As he picked up what he thought was dirt and threw it into the trash can.

I yelled at him, "Lieutenant, that's not dirt. That's a piece of shrapnel I got out of my right arm. They missed it in the hospital in Da Nang. It festered up like a pimple. I squeezed it and this little piece of shrapnel popped out."

"Man, I'm sorry."

"Don't worry about it. There it is. I'm gonna see if the nurse has any tape. I'll just tape it to the inside of the box."

The lieutenant left. The nurse got me tape so I wouldn't lose that little piece of metal.

Our flight landed outside Anchorage where elementary school kids waited for us just outside the officers' mess. Each of us wounded had a young boy or girl assigned to us. They carried our food trays, got us each something cold to drink, and sat beside us.

It was hard to say who was more nervous, me or the young man assigned to me. The scar on my head was clearly visible. When I glanced toward him, he looked away or down. The boy was probably eleven or twelve. He made me feel special. I would be forever grateful to him.

Landing at Millington, we were taken to the hospital. There was no air conditioning in the hospital but luckily it was the second week of September. It was just outside Memphis. It was warm but manageable. The Marine liaison told me the Corps would try to get me as close to my hometown as possible.

At my first meeting with the neurosurgeon, he told me it would be at least another month before my surgery. I needed more time for my wound to heal. He told me the date he was shooting for would be the middle or maybe late October.

My stepfather's family was having a reunion in October in Houston. I always got along well with his brothers and sister, so I asked for basket leave and got it. Having grown up in Houston, I was anxious to call and talk to several people, some of which I hadn't seen in three or four years.

After landing, I walked through the concourse until I spotted my ol' man. We greeted each other as if we were actually glad to see one another. He drove to Uncle Jack's house. As I got there, glancing out the window, looking at the people going about their lives, I realized the war had little effect on them, if any. All they knew was what they saw on the evening news or in the newspaper.

That night, I made calls and drove over to talk to old friends. It felt good to sit and talk and to listen. For a few moments, it felt like I had never left.

After three days, I was back at the airport, flying back to Memphis, then to Millington and surgery on my head. As I was being prepped on the table, the doctor came up to me.

"Good luck, Doc."

"Just lie there and take a deep breath."

The lights once again went out. When I woke up, it was so hot sweat ran down my face. My head was throbbing.

"Nurse can you give me something? My head is killing me."

"I'll check with the doctor. Just hang on for a minute."

Moments later she was back, gave me a shot, and moved my bed closer to the screen door. There was no air conditioning. It was October just outside Memphis. The humidity was high. I looked around and passed out.

For several days I stayed in bed, only getting up with the help of the corpsman to go to the head. As the days turned to weeks, I got my strength back and even gained weight.

After the bandages came off, the doctor came by to check his handy work. After what seemed like a lot of 'uh huh' and 'that's nice', all seemed to be in good order except for one place at the base of my skull. It wasn't healing like he thought it should.

At some point I asked him, "Doc, can I play ball again?"

"I don't know. I'm concerned about that one place at the base of your skull. Now over time, your skull will eventually grow in the plate. It will be stronger than any part of your skull."

* * *

Over the next few months, I began to feel like my old self, going to the gym, working out, gaining weight.

It was December, 1968. I drove up to Miami, Oklahoma. Northeastern Oklahoma A&M was one of the finest junior colleges in the country. Its football program was unparalleled. A lot of Division

One schools looked for talent there. I would tell the coach my time in the Corps was coming to an end. All I wanted was a chance to try out, get through spring ball, work out over the summer, and get ready for fall. I was determined to make it.

I met with the head coach, Chuck Bowman.

He told me, "I can't offer you a scholarship 'til I see you play."

"That's fine with me, Coach. All I want is a chance to play. I will get out of the Corps mid-January. I'll drive up and start my classes."

"Good, we'll see you then. You check in with the coach at the jock dorm. He'll have a room for you."

"Thanks, Coach. I'll see you next month."

Turning to leave, I looked back and smiled. I walked across the campus. It felt I belonged there. I was home.

Finishing up my paperwork, I left the Corps as a corporal, grabbed my bag, and headed out the door. A staff sergeant offered me a ride to the airport. He said it was practically on his way.

I said very little to him as we drove. My thoughts were with the past, the young men I had gone through boot camp with, how many had made it through Vietnam...Would our paths cross again? Probably not.

When I came into this world a 'black cloud' hung over me. That was all over. God had seen fit to give me a second chance. I didn't like having to deceive Coach Bowman, but I knew if I told him about my head, he would never have given me a chance. It was important to me. Going into the Corps was the point to gain weight, maturity, become a better person, a better man.

So what if I had a hole in my head?

It's like my uncle said, "You've got a hard head. If they had hit you anywhere else, it would have killed you."

I was not married. My only responsibility was to myself. I would see it through—throw the dice.

10

"COACH, JB'S BRAINS ARE FALLING OUT!"

If you want to be a rock be a precious stone. ~ Vietnamese Proverb

AVING SETTLED INTO MY CLASSES, college life was easy to get used to. I walked across campus. It seemed so quiet, people going by. They were completely oblivious to what was going on halfway around the world. In Vietnam, young men were setting in ambush sites, manning the wire, peering into the darkness, watching, listening, waiting for a sign. Death was out there, and he was hungry.

My roommate was Gary Vance, a very likable person. He was a sophomore, so it was his last semester at NEO. Football was starting up in a few days. My bench, squat, and dead-lift were all good. I tried to run on the track every other day. There was no problem with my head except for a little drainage on the left side at the base of my skull. It always healed up then started to drain again. My body had accepted the plate except for that one spot.

I liked Gary. I had come to trust him. The night before practice we were both studying in our room.

"Gary, I need to talk to you. I need to tell you something but before I do, I want your word you won't tell another soul."

"Okay, man, you got it. What's so important?"

"When I was in Vietnam, I had a grenade go off next to me. It hit me in my right arm, both legs, my butt, and in the head. I lost about two square inches of my skull. They put a plastic plate in my head. Nobody knows anything about it but you. There's nothing to worry about but if I did go down, I know you'll be out there watching us practice. I want you to say something if I don't get up. Then at least they'll know what to look for. All right, are we good?"

"Yeah, I'll be out there. You can trust me. I won't say a word."

"Your word?"

"My word."

For the first week things seemed to be all right. I had headaches but then I always had headaches.

During the second week, my head began to drain more. I took several paper towels to class with me to dab and wipe off my neck. I tried to do it as inconspicuously as possible, not to let anyone notice.

It had been almost two weeks. Practice was over, and we headed for the locker room. My head hurt.

The insulation on the inside of my helmet rubbed against my scar. I dragged my feet and waited until everyone but me had headed to the showers.

I went to the trainer's room and grabbed scissors. As I sat in front of my locker, I took the scissors and cut and tore out the insulation on that side of my helmet. Having just started, I heard a noise. I looked up.

Coach Tiger stood there.

"What are you doing to one of my helmets?"

I looked at him, took a deep breath, and leaned back on my locker. There wasn't much I could say.

In my heart, I knew I was through. The headaches were getting worse. The drainage wouldn't stop. It didn't matter how bad I wanted it. My playing days were over, and I knew it.

"Coach, there's something I need to tell you."

Sitting there, I told him about the grenade, the plate in my head, and the drainage.

He suddenly reached down and grabbed my arm and stood me up. He led me to Coach Bowman's office.

I still had my football shoes on, so I felt like I was ice skating across the concrete floor on my steel-tipped nylon cleats.

Coach Tiger turned the doorknob and threw open the door. "Coach, JB's brains are falling out!"

"Come in, take a seat and tell me about it."

The three of us sat there as I told them about my head, that I was certain if I had told them, they would not have let me try. It was important to me. As I got older, I didn't want to look back and wonder if I could have made it.

"And now you know."

* * *

A few days later, I left for Oklahoma City and the VA hospital. During surgery, they put packing under my scalp to fight infection and a tube coming out of my head that drained onto a towel on my left shoulder.

I wanted to go outside, feel the sun on my face but the foyer downstairs was as far as I got.

Then one afternoon, I was walking around in the hallway, looking outside toward the back of the hospital. Through the window, I saw a group of young boys playing softball.

Wearing my pajamas, a blue robe, and showers shoes, I took the elevator to the ground floor. Buttoning up my robe, I snuck out the back.

With the sun in my face, I walked to the field. As I got closer, practically every one of the boys had some sort of attachment on their ears. They were from a special school just beyond the fence. A young man was obviously in charge.

As I neared the field, I hollered at him, "Can I play?"

"Sure, take second."

That was a big moment for me. I hadn't been that happy for some time. The kids got up to bat, the young man lobbed the ball to them. They stayed at the plate as long as it took to get a hit.

I had forgotten about my head. Those kids were great medicine for me.

Then suddenly, "Are they looking for you?" The kid pointed.

I turned back toward the hospital. Standing there were two male nurses. One of them was motioning for me to come on. I looked back at the kids.

"Thanks a lot. I enjoyed it!" Turning, I walked toward my two jailers. "You two really messed up a good time. How'd you know I was out here?"

"Someone saw you from a window and called us."

The next morning when the doctor made his rounds, he said, "I hear you escaped to the ball field."

"Yeah, Doc. But I didn't get to stay long. Someone spotted me and sent a couple of male nurses to go get me."

"I can certainly sympathize with you, but you need to stay inside until we close that opening in your head. There's always the chance of more infection."

"Okay, Doc."

A couple of days went by. Sometimes I just stood at the window and watched the kids play on the field. Somehow a tennis ball found its way into my hands. I took it out back and played catch with myself, bouncing it off the wall and being careful to stay close to the building. Anyone looking out a window wasn't likely to see me. Staying out there for hours, no one came for me again.

I healed up. The doctors released me, and I headed back to NEO. It had been about a month since I left school. Hopefully, the professors would let me make up the work. I first had to find Coach Bowman, talk to him, and somehow try to make him understand.

Heading for the practice field, I saw Coach Bowman. He looked up and saw me. There was a big smile on his face.

"Coach Bowman."

"Hello JB. It's good to see you."

"Listen Coach, I feel like I owe you an apology. I know it was wrong to deceive you. But you've got to understand, it was important for me. I had to try."

"I do understand, but from here on when I get a young man out of the military, I'm gonna have him checked from the top of his head to the bottom of his feet."

"Coach, I know that my playing days are over, but I would like to stay with the team. Maybe you could see your way to letting me be a trainer or a manager?"

"JB, I'll tell you, you tell me what you want to do. The choice is yours."

"A trainer, Coach. That's what I want, to be a trainer."

"Then it's settled. The job's yours."

"Thanks, Coach. I've got to go and talk to my professors about the work I missed."

He waved me on. My professors agreed to let me make up the work, even my history professor, Coach Tiger.

* * *

In June of '69, I was in the hayfield bucking hay bales with Norma and Brad. After work I felt the back of my head, that same spot at the base of my skull. It was draining again.

When I put pressure on the plate, it felt spongy—the same way it felt before my other surgeries. I mentioned it to Norma.

She felt bad, thinking it had something to do with being in the hayfields, working and sweating. Before I left, I assured her it had nothing to do with hard work. I told her that one spot below the plate had never healed right since my second surgery at Millington.

When I got in touch with the VA, they set up a date for an appointment. After the neurologist examined my skull, a date was set for my fourth operation.

I was in the hospital for three weeks. After surgery, they again packed my head with an antibiotic cloth and a drain tube. The doctor pulled out the cloth every morning through a slit in my skin, then pack the hole with a new cloth.

It was very painful.

The infection was finally gone. I could go home with the understanding if it started draining again I was to call and keep the doctor informed.

In August, just a few weeks before football was to start, it started draining again.

Talking to my doctor, who by the way had a great sense of humor told me, "JB, I don't think your body is going to accept that plate. If we keep this up, we're going to have to put a zipper in the back of your head."

It was understandable. I, too, was getting tired of all the surgeries.

A date was set. They would remove the plastic plate. Nothing would cover my brain but skin and hair. That meant I would be late for football. I was sure Coach Bowman would understand. It was important to me to be a part of the team.

A couple of days before my surgery, a doctor came into the hospital bay. Walking up to my bed and looking at my charts, he said, "You don't remember me, do you?"

"No, sir. I don't."

"I'm the one who did the first surgery on you in Da Nang."

"I'm sorry I didn't recognize you." We had only met a couple of times. It never occurred to me we would cross paths again. "Thanks, Doc."

He left.

I began thinking what were the odds he did the first surgery in Da Nang. And he was there in Oklahoma City at the VA hospital. It felt good knowing he was the one who would be removing the plate.

After the surgery, I was in my bed with my head wrapped up. For the first day, they had me pretty well doped up. I gained consciousness, woke up, looked around, and passed out again.

It reminded me a lot of my first surgery, except they kept me covered up and there wasn't a nun sitting at my side.

The second day, my doctor dropped by.

"I wasn't sure you would be awake. Yesterday I came by. You said a few words then passed out.

"Your surgery went well. Part of your skull had grown into the plastic plate. We had to remove a little more of your skull to get it out. You bled quite a bit but that was to be expected. Your skin had stretched enough we didn't have to use wire sutures this time.

"All-in-all, I think you came through the surgery quite well. You will probably be able to leave the hospital in about two weeks. I'll want to see you back here in about a month. After that, you can let your hair grow out. Is there anything you would like to ask me?"

"No, Doc. I think you've covered everything. Thank you."

I left the hospital and headed home for a short visit then I drove to Miami, Oklahoma and NEO.

Practice had started. It felt good to be back in school. I felt a little self-conscious about my head. The scars were clearly visible because my hair hadn't grown out enough to cover them.

Nobody ever said anything, but I felt their eyes on me as I walked to class.

As the season progressed, I felt a real closeness to the players and coaches. I taped the players' ankles and hands, took care of their scrapes, and put them into the whirlpool for sore muscles.

It was a great season. NEO played Arizona Western for the National Championship in Savannah, Georgia. After winning the game, the team flew back to Miami where a large crowd waited.

Four members of the team made All American. Two went to the University of Oklahoma. One went to Alabama. One went to the University of Tulsa. Other players on the team went to Texas A&M, Baylor, Iowa State, University of Cincinnati, University of Louisville, and Wake Forest.

At the football banquet there were coaches from Oklahoma, Oklahoma State University, and Alabama. I met and shook hands with Bear Bryant.

Every year the team voted on the Monty Franks Spirit Award. It could be awarded to anyone on the team.

Coach Bowman stood up in a team meeting and explained to everyone what the award meant. Everyone was eligible, players, coaches, managers, or trainers.

I wanted to win the award, but I put down someone else's name. If I won, I wanted it to be because the team wanted me to have it, not because I voted for myself.

During the banquet, Coach Tiger stood up and explained what the Spirit Award meant.

I kept eating. If he didn't call out my name, I would put down my fork and stand and clap. No one would know of my disappointment.

"This year the Monty Franks Spirit Award goes to JB Redus."

One of the players at our table hollered, "JB, it's you! It's you! Stand up!"

I rose out of my chair and headed for the coaches' table.

Coach Tiger leaned over and handed me the trophy with a big smile and a firm handshake. "Congratulations, JB."

"Thanks, Coach."

J. B. Redus receives the Monty Franks Spirit Award.

Coach Tiger handing JB his award at NEO 1969 football Banquet, Monty Franks Spirit Award

* * *

157

A few weeks later I learned I had been accepted to the University of Tulsa on a training scholarship. Being at NEO was just what I needed after Vietnam. The players and coaches accepted me—made me feel like a part of the team. I was one of them.

* * *

One day in early October 1969, I noticed a girl walking with friends in front of the cafeteria. At the time, I was several stories above the ground, looking out a large window.

Asking one of the people in the room, I got her name. I managed to have lunch with her the next day.

JB and Cherry, 2009

I married that girl. We've been together for fifty-one years.

For all we have said and not said,
For all we have thought and not thought,
For all we have done and not done.
May God forgive us. ~ Zorro

EPILOGUE

"...if men have a common factor, it seems to me it's their ability to err. If a man's mistakes determine what he was, then what he does about those mistakes should determine what he is." Paladin; Have Gun–Will Travel (television series)

IN NOVEMBER 1968, THE NATION was going to elect a new President. LBJ told the American people he would not seek and he would not accept his party's nomination of President. The Democrats chose Hubert Humphrey. The Republicans chose Richard Nixon—a man who would do anything not to lose that election.

President Johnson, during his last few months in office was trying to bring both North and South Vietnam to Paris in an effort to stop the war. Johnson and Nixon had known each other for years when they both served in the US Senate. Johnson didn't like Nixon. He didn't trust Nixon.

During the two months prior to the election, Nixon did all he could to undermine the peace treaty. In his mind, if the Democrats were successful, it could cost him the election.

A woman named Anna Chennault, wife of General Clare Chennault—the famous leader of the Flying Tigers during China's war with Japan—worked with Nixon. She was widely known as the Steel Butterfly. She made several trips to South Vietnam on behalf of Nixon to inform President Thieu he would get a better deal with Nixon as the US President than with the Democrats.

Just days before the election, the North Vietnamese agreed to meet in Paris but through the influence of Anna Chennault, the South Vietnamese refused to participate. Johnson tapped the phone lines of the South Vietnamese Embassy.

Using words like treason and collusion, Johnson had the goods on Nixon. He had the proof he needed to expose Nixon to the nation just before the election.

Talking to the people he trusted—the wise men around him—they agreed not to make it public. The information they had, had come from the NSA, FBI, and CIA. It was picked up through classified, sensitive sources.

LBJ felt that, "If you start putting this kind of information into elections, that's going to change what kind of country we have."

After the peace talks were shut down in 1968, there were five more years of war. It cost the lives of over thirty thousand more Americans.

Johnson put the information he had into an envelope, marked with an X file. It was not to be opened for fifty years.

* * *

In Washington DC, a wall of black marble lists the names of the men and women who made the ultimate sacrifice.

It is a solemn place. People speak in soft voices or whisper when they visit.

Witness the names—how overwhelming it can be.

To this day, the war still casts a long shadow to some. They will remember nothing except we were strangers in a strange land.

Don't forget your handkerchief.

Semper Fi

> The new orders do not deny the necessity of an active defense, but they would scale down the massive search-and-destroy missions that have dominated U.S. strategy. Said one Government official: "Where we used to have division-sized sweeps, we now want to see whether the job can't be done by 25-man patrols. Where we now send out 25-man patrols, we want to see whether a five-man patrol won't do. And we must keep in mind that we are no longer out for military victory." The new approach also calls for increased Vietnamization of the war. U.S. troops would spend less time in combat and far more time training ARVN. Obviously, both proposals are designed to cut U.S. casualties.

Excerpt from "The Nation"
July 1969 issue of Time Magazine

ABOUT THE AUTHOR

James Bruce Redus was born in Shawnee, Oklahoma in 1947. His family moved to Houston, Texas after he was born. JB attended Kelso Elementary and Spring Branch Junior High. He attended Memorial High School in Houston.

His family moved to Tulsa, Oklahoma halfway through his junior year. He finished high school, graduating from Memorial High School in Tulsa in 1965.

* * *

JB enlisted in the Marine Corps in 1966. Boot camp was at MCRD in San Diego. His platoon was 2238.

After that, he went to Sea School with twenty-nine other Marines. He graduated at the head of his class.

He became a Flag Marine in early March of 1967. He served as a Flag Marine on the USS *St. Paul* and the *Newport News*. Both ships were deployed off the coast of North Vietnam in the Gulf of Tonkin.

JB transferred to the 2nd Battalion 5th Marines 1st Marine Division, Golf Company. His MOS was 0300; basic rifleman.

He was wounded by a Chi Com grenade on July 28, 1968 in Vietnam.

After multiple surgeries on his head in Vietnam, Memphis, Tennessee and Tulsa, Oklahoma, he enrolled in NEO Junior College in Miami, Oklahoma to complete his Associate Degree.

* * *

He met his wife, Cherry at NEO. They were married in 1970.

He is the proud father of four children: Brady, Rachel, Cherry Beth and Megan.

He has eight grandchildren and now lives in Cleora, Oklahoma.

JB with his daughters, Megan, Rachel, and Cherry Beth.